BEST OF

Mumbai

Joe Bindloss

How to use this book

Colour-Coding & Maps

Each chapter has a colour code along the banner at the top of the page which is also used for text and symbols on maps (eg all venues reviewed in the Highlights chapter are orange on the maps). The fold-out maps inside the front and back covers are numbered from 1 to 5. All sights and venues in the text have map references; eg, (3, C3) means Map 3, grid reference C3. See p96 for map symbols.

Prices

Multiple prices listed with reviews (eg Rs 35/20) usually indicate adult/concession admission to a venue. Concession prices can include senior, student, member or coupon discounts. Meal cost and room rate categories are listed at the start of the Eating and Sleeping chapters, respectively.

Text Symbols

- ☎ telephone
- ✉ address
- 🖳 email/website address
- $ admission
- 🕑 opening hours
- ⓘ information
- 🚢 ferry
- 🚆 train
- ♿ wheelchair access
- ✗ on site/nearby eatery

Best of Mumbai
1st edition – February 2006

Published by Lonely Planet Publications Pty Ltd
ABN 36 005 607 983

Australia Head Office, Locked Bag 1, Footscray, Vic 3011
   ☎ 03 8379 8000 fax 03 8379 8111
   🖳 talk2us@lonelyplanet.com.au
USA 150 Linden St, Oakland, CA 94607
   ☎ 510 893 8555 toll free 800 275 8555
   fax 510 893 8572
   🖳 info@lonelyplanet.com
UK 72–82 Rosebery Avenue, London EC1R 4RW
   ☎ 020 7841 9000 fax 020 7841 9001
   🖳 go@lonelyplanet.co.uk

This title was commissioned in Lonely Planet's Melbourne office and produced by: **Commissioning Editor** Janine Eberle **Coordinating Editor** Kate Whitfield **Layout Designer** Kaitlin Beckett **Editors** Laura Gibb, Helen Christinis, Kate Evans **Cartographers** Sarah Sloane, Andrew Smith, David Connolly, Jolyon Philcox, Valentina Kremenchutskaya, Joshua Geoghegan, Owen Eszeki **Managing Cartographer** Shahara Ahmed **Cover Designer** Rebecca Dandens **Project Managers** Glenn van der Knijff, Sarah Sloane **Mapping Development** Paul Piaia **Desktop Publishing Support** Mark Germanchis **Thanks to** Julie Sheridan, Chris LeeAck, Lachlan Ross, Suzannah Shwer, Darren O'Connell, Gabrielle Wilson, Brigitte Ellemor, Jacqui Saunders

© Lonely Planet Publications Pty Ltd 2006.

Photographs by Lonely Planet Images and Mick Elmore except for the following: p5, p11, p14, p17, p22, p24, p29 (top), p35, p36, p37 Joe Bindloss, p25, p67 David Collins, p19 Dallas Stribley. **Cover photograph** Portrait of the famous Ganesha of Lal Baug in Mumbai, Hira Punjabi/Lonely Planet Images.

All images are copyright of the photographers unless otherwise indicated. Many of the images in this guide are available for licensing from Lonely Planet Images: www.lonelyplanetimages.com.

ISBN 1 74104 737 4

Printed through The Bookmaker International Ltd.
Printed in China

Contents

From the Publisher

AUTHOR
Joe Bindloss

Joe first got hooked on India in the early '90s and he's been visiting regularly to satisfy his chai and biryani habit ever since. Joe was born in Cyprus, grew up in England and has lived and worked in half a dozen countries, though he currently calls London home. When he isn't working on guidebooks, Joe writes for newspapers and magazines in the UK and indulges his climbing and Xbox habits.

I credit my work on this book to Peg Southgate. Thanks also to my partner Linda Nylind for steadfast support. In Mumbai, thanks to the staff at the Sea Shore Hotel and Bentley's Hotel. Staff at the India Tourism office and Times of India also provided invaluable assistance.

LONELY PLANET AUTHORS

Why is our travel information the best in the world? It's simple: our authors are independent, dedicated travellers. They don't research using just the Internet or phone, and they don't take freebies in exchange for positive coverage. They travel widely, to all the popular spots and off the beaten track. They personally visit thousands of hotels, restaurants, cafés, bars, galleries, palaces, museums and more – and they take pride in getting all the details right, and telling it how it is. For more, see the authors section on **www.lonelyplanet.com**.

PHOTOGRAPHER
Mick Elmore

When he was five Mick Elmore borrowed his older brother's camera and started taking pictures of family, friends, pets, and then holidays. His passion became his profession after university when Mick became a journalist on the Mexican border in Texas in 1984. Since then his cameras – mostly Nikon – have taken him around the world, with longer stays in Guatemala, Colombia, Australia, Cambodia and Thailand, where has now been based for 10 years. Mick started selling photos to Lonely Planet in the early '90s and has been part of Lonely Planet Images team since its beginning.

Introducing Mumbai

When British Governor Gerald Aungier set up camp on Bombay island in 1672, he probably had no idea what he was about to create. Fast forward two hundred years and Bombay (now Mumbai) is India's 'Maximum City', bold, brash, fast and frenetic, always faddish, fashion-obsessed and undeniably animated in all aspects of its life.

Three centuries of development have transformed seven scrubby islands into a mighty metropolis of towering apartment blocks, colonial mansions, seafront promenades and air-conditioned shopping malls. If Delhi is the seat of history and Kolkata the seat of culture, Mumbai is the address of film and fashion – many leading designers are based here and the Bollywood movie machine churns out a staggering 1000 films a year.

Mumbai is where Indian fantasies of wealth and glamour engage in a bizarre dance with poverty and slums, and where economic boom flirts with social collapse. More than 60% of Mumbaikers live in shanty-towns, yet the city also boasts some of the most expensive real estate in the country. Plans are afoot to build a futuristic new town of towering skyscrapers in the north of the city, transforming Mumbai into the Shanghai of India.

From a visitor's perspective, Mumbai is a place to shop and dine by day and party by night. Bring your cheque book, plenty of baggage allowance and some Alka-Seltzer for the morning after.

Hold on tight; Mumbai is fast-paced and fabulous

Neighbourhoods

Mumbai's neighbourhoods broadly follow the outlines of the seven islands that were joined to create the modern city. There is a noticeable north–south divide – most historic and cultural offerings are in south Mumbai, while bars, shops and malls are concentrated in the north.

In the south, **Colaba** is one of the oldest parts of Mumbai and the main tourist precinct. There are hotels in all price ranges, excellent places to eat and drink and a lively but not overpowering traveller scene. This is also the starting point for the boat trip to **Elephanta Island**. North of Colaba, K Dubash Marg (Rampart Row) in Kala Ghoda has some of Mumbai's finest restaurants.

Further north is **Fort**, the heart of old British Bombay. This was the original banking and commercial quarter and the streets are lined with museums, galleries and emporiums. Fort's **Dr DN Road** is lined with banks and historic buildings.

> ### OFF THE BEATEN TRACK
> To escape the crowds, leave Colaba and head into the back alleys of Fort or the maze of alleys north of Crawford Market. Another serene area to wander around is Malabar Hill. To *really* escape the crowds, head to Sanjay Gandhi National Park (p35).

At the north end of Fort is **Victoria Terminus** (Chhatrapati Shivaji Terminus; CST), Mumbai's main train station, and further on are the market districts of **Kalbadevi** and **Bhuleshwar,** and the **Chor Bazaar** bric-a-brac market. Running alongside Fort are two huge parks, the **Oval Maidan** and the **Azad Maidan**. Further west you'll find **Nariman Point**, home to most of the embassies and airline offices, and **Churchgate**, a smart neighbourhood of upmarket restaurants.

From Nariman Point, Marine Dr (Netaji Subhashchandra Bose Marg) runs north to famous **Chowpatty Beach** and the parks of **Malabar Hill**. Further north is **Breach Candy**, home to upmarket boutiques, and **Mahalaxmi**, the setting for Mumbai's dhobi ghats and the Haji Ali Dargah. Just north is home to the Phoenix Mills Shopping Centre.

On the north side of Mahim Creek, **Bandra** is Mumbai's premier shopping, dining and nightlife district – Linking Rd is the heart of the action. Nearby **Juhu Beach** is a continuous string of luxury beachfront hotels and due east is **Andheri**, with the international and domestic airports and airport hotels.

Fast tracks, bright lights, big city

Many of Mumbai's streets have two names; a colonial name and a post-Independence one. For more information on street names, see p83.

Itineraries

Planning your time in Mumbai will depend on what you want to achieve. For culture and history, concentrate on south Mumbai. If you came here for shoes and accessories, head north to Bandra or Phoenix Mills in Lower Parel.

Other big activities in Mumbai are dining (best experienced in Colaba, Fort, Churchgate and Bandra) and drinking (the slickest nightspots are in Colaba, Bandra, Lower Parel and Andheri).

WORST OF MUMBAI
- Beggars and hangers-on along Colaba Causeway
- The fishy pong from Sassoon Docks when the wind blows north
- The lack of information at the Maharashtra Tourism Development Corporation (MTDC) tourist office
- The price of a Kingfisher beer at upmarket Mumbai restaurants

SOUTH MUMBAI SHUFFLE (ONE DAY)
With just one day it makes sense to stick to south Mumbai. Explore the street market on Colaba Causeway (Shahid Bhagat Singh Marg) and visit one of Fort's galleries or museums. Shop for souvenirs in the emporiums on Dr DN Rd and dine at Khyber, Mumbai's best restaurant.

NORTH & SOUTH (TWO DAYS)
With two days, give half a day each to Fort and Colaba. Start with the Chhatrapati Shivaji Maharaj Museum then explore the historic buildings and emporiums of Fort. Detour north to Chowpatty for a plate of *bhelpuri* (Mumbai-style salad), followed by a sit-down dinner at one of the dining spots on K Dubash Marg (Rampart Row). On day two ride the suburban train to Bandra and shop your way along Linking Rd. After lunch, take your pick of the Mani Bhavan museum near Chowpatty or the Haji Ali Dargah near Breach Candy.

CULTURE, HISTORY & SHOPPING (THREE DAYS)
With three days you can venture further afield. On the first day catch some culture at Colaba's museums and galleries and some history on Fort's Dr DN Rd. Stroll north to Crawford Market and the alleys of Chor Bazaar. Day two is shopping day – start on Colaba Causeway, head north to Dr DN Rd in Fort, then browse the boutiques of Bandra. Finish the day with dinner and cocktails on nearby Waterfield Rd. Set aside day three to visit Elephanta Island. With any time left over, wander south to Sassoon Docks or take in a Bollywood blockbuster at the Regal Cinema in Colaba.

Bustle and balloons, Gateway of India (p12)

Highlights

ELEPHANTA ISLAND (1, B3)

Surrounded by oil refineries and supertankers in the middle of Mumbai Harbour, the tiny island of Elephanta is home to Mumbai's most important historical attraction. Carved into the basalt bedrock of the island is a series of Hindu caves containing some of the finest temple carvings in India. This is easily the most popular tourist sight in Mumbai and thousands of visitors flock here daily to admire the carvings and enjoy the leisurely boat ride across Mumbai Harbour.

INFORMATION

- ✉ Elephanta Island, Mumbai Harbour
- 💲 Indian/foreigner Rs 10/250 plus tax per adult/child Rs 5/3, video camera Rs 25
- 🕙 9am-5.30pm Tue-Sun
- ℹ English guide booklet available (Rs 50); deluxe boat tickets include free guided tour
- 🚢 ferries from Gateway of India 9am-2.30pm; last return to Mumbai 5.30pm
- 🍴 MTDC-run Chalukya Restaurant

Hindu rock carvings on Elephanta Island

The main temple on Elephanta is a fascinating honeycomb of shrines, caverns, open courtyards and prayer halls, created by the Maurya civilisation in the 6th century. The interior of the cave was once painted with colourful frescoes but centuries of erosion have reduced the paintings to a few dabs of turquoise and ochre on the walls.

The centrepiece of the temple is a monumental statue of **Mahesh-Murti** (Trimurti), depicting Shiva as the creator, preserver and destroyer of the universe. The statue has three faces, each as tall as a double-decker bus. In the centre is Shiva the creator, with a magnificent jewelled headdress and a look of serene contemplation, flanked by Vamdeo (the feminine, preserving incarnation of Shiva) and Rudra (the destroyer of the universe).

Many of the other carvings around the cave temple were damaged by the Portuguese, but the statue of Shiva as **Nataraja**, dancing the divine dance that created the universe, is still very impressive. Uphill from the main temple are three smaller caves with unfinished carvings. By the entrance to the archaeological zone is a small **museum** containing sculptures rescued from around the island.

THE ELEPHANT OF ELEPHANTA

Elephanta Island was originally known as Gharapuri (fortress of the Shaivite priests), but Portuguese explorers renamed the island after discovering a massive stone elephant on the shore. The elephant of Elephanta survived a hundred years of Portuguese rule (quite an achievement considering that Portuguese soldiers used the 'heathen' carvings on Elephanta for target practice!) but the statue finally succumbed to erosion in 1814. The elephant was later rescued by British archaeologists who reassembled the pieces next to the Dr Bhau Daji Lad Museum (p21) in Byculla.

The cave is a 2km hike from the jetty along a causeway lined with monkeys and stalls selling religious paraphernalia. A miniature steam train covers half the distance for Rs 8 and you can hire a 'dolly' (sedan chair) for the final stage up to the cave for Rs 200/300 one way/return. Local guides offer their services in exchange for tips; you'll find them near the entrance to the archaeological zone.

Boats to Elephanta leave from the Gateway of India, but the boat operators pool their profits so there's no advantage to choosing one company over another. Visitors have the choice of economy boats with few creature comforts for Rs 90 or 'deluxe' boats with soft-drink vendors, padded seats and a free guided tour on arrival for Rs 110. Services are reduced during the monsoon.

Be warned: Elephanta can get extremely crowded, especially at weekends. To escape the crowds, hike up the hill opposite the main cave. Hidden away in the forest are several unadorned cave temples, a ruined Buddhist stupa and plenty of peaceful serenity. The trail begins below the entrance to the main Elephanta temple, near the abandoned forestry booth.

DON'T MISS
- The awesome Mahesh-Murti statue
- Elephanta's famous dancing Nataraja
- The sculpture museum
- Hiking up Elephanta's eastern hill

Monkeys doing business at Elephanta Island

An illustrated guide booklet on Elephanta is available from stalls on the way up to the main temple for Rs 50. Con artists near the Gateway of India sell the same booklet for Rs 250. More interesting is the Elephanta comic book (Rs 75), published by Amar Chitra Katha, which explains the colourful legends behind the carvings at Elephanta.

Every February, Elephanta holds a two-day festival of music and dance in the courtyards of the main temple (p68) and boats run late into the evening to ferry visitors back to the mainland.

CHOWPATTY BEACH (3, B3)

At the northern end of Marine Dr (Netaji Subhashchandra Bose Marg), by the foot of Malabar Hill, Chowpatty Beach is probably the most famous location in Mumbai. This long, sweeping beach has acted as the backdrop to a dozen Bollywood movies. Generations of Mumbaikers have grown up promenading along the sands and munching on plates of spicy *bhelpuri* (Mumbai-style salad). When India rebelled against British rule, this was where the crowds gathered to chant 'Jai Hind' (Victory to India) and drive home the case for Indian independence.

INFORMATION

- ✉ Chowpatty Seaface, Chowpatty
- 🚉 Charni Road
- 🍴 *bhelpuri* stands (p55) or restaurants on Chowpatty Seaface (p55)

Chowpatty used to be rather run down, but the beach received a thorough make-over in the late 1990s and the new-look Chowpatty boasts an impressively litter-free strip of golden sand, patrolled by lifeguards and lit up at night by giant strip lights. By day couples gather to contemplate the splashing waves, and by night the beach becomes Mumbai's main venue for a leisurely stroll.

Visiting Chowpatty at night is an essential part of any trip to Mumbai. A carnival atmosphere pervades, and local families come together to walk, talk, eat and promenade along the sands. Hand-operated fairground rides are set up for children, and *malish*-wallahs (masseurs) stalk the sands looking for suitable victims to pummel.

The liveliest time to visit Chowpatty is during the annual **Ganesh Chaturthi festival** (p68), a time when hundreds of clay effigies of the elephant-headed god are ritually immersed in the ocean, accompanied by huge amounts of water throwing, dancing and music. Enormous cranes are brought down onto the beach to handle the largest effigies. It's an incredible spectacle, though it probably contributes to the ongoing pollution problems in Back Bay.

REINVENTING CHOWPATTY

Swimming might be the last thing on your mind when you visit Chowpatty Beach, but Mumbaikers are taking to the sea in ever-increasing numbers, paddling, sailing and even swimming in the warm, murky waters of the Arabian Sea. We can't vouch for the cleanliness of the water, but if you fancy joining them, a whole range of watersports can be arranged at **H₂O** (p30) on Chowpatty Beach.

Sunset session, Chowpatty Beach

VICTORIA TERMINUS (4, E2)

If there ever was a building that summed up a city, it would be Victoria Terminus. This extravagant Victorian-Gothic fantasy falls somewhere between Notre Dame and the Taj Mahal, with a hint of fairy-tale castle thrown in for good measure. Travel writer Jan Morris once described it as 'the central building of the entire British Empire' – not bad for a municipal train station in the middle of Mumbai.

This glorious architectural confection was created in 1887 by architect Frederick Stevens, a pioneer of the so-called 'hybrid' style, which borrowed heavily from mosque and temple architecture. From here, the steam trains of the Great Indian Peninsular Railway Company fanned out across the nation, extending as far as Delhi, Kolkata and Chennai.

Victoria Terminus is still Mumbai's largest and busiest train station, though many long-distance services now leave from Mumbai Central. After Independence, the station was renamed Chhatrapati Shivaji Terminus (CST) in honour of the famous Maratha hero, but most locals still refer to it as 'VT'. It's worth coming here even if you don't plan to make a train journey, particularly around lunchtime, when hundreds of tiffin-wallahs arrive from the suburbs carrying packed lunches for Mumbai's office workers.

INFORMATION

- ✉ cnr Dr DN Rd & Nagar Chowk, Fort
- $ free
- ⌚ 24hr
- 🚇 CST
- 🍴 fast-food counters inside the station

Fairy-tale extravagance; Victoria Terminus

The building is fabulous overall, but be sure to get up close and admire the detail. The entire exterior is covered with carvings, statues, turrets and domes. Dog-faced gargoyles jut from the **central tower** and graceful peacock and lyrebird windows look out over the central courtyard. Some of the most elegant ornamentation was saved for the **reservation office** – check out the carvings of mongooses, monkeys, pangolins and other native fauna in the porch.

DON'T MISS

- The magnificent central tower
- Peacock windows on the main courtyard
- Gargoyles on the reservation office porch
- Tiffin-wallahs at midday

GATEWAY OF INDIA AND TAJ MAHAL PALACE & TOWER (5, C2)

It's rather ironic that Mumbai's most famous landmark was built for a one-off visit by a foreign monarch. Set on the quayside at the end of Apollo Bunder, the grand Gateway of India was constructed in 1924 to commemorate a state visit by King George V. The arch was intended as a monument to the enduring nature of the British Empire, but just 24 years later the last British soldiers marched through the gateway to waiting boats as India stepped forward to Independence.

INFORMATION

✉ Apollo Bunder, Colaba

💲 free

🕓 24hr

🚉 Churchgate

🍴 Golden Dragon (p50) or Colaba restaurants (p49)

Architecturally the Gateway is a classic triumphal arch, but the style and decoration borrows heavily from 16th-century Gujarati architecture. Standing alone on the quayside, it looks like the gateway to a Mughal city that never was. Try to visit in the late afternoon, when the light brings out the colours of the yellow basalt.

This was the point of arrival for thousands of British sahibs and memsahibs (gentlemen and gentlewomen) but the Gateway has been firmly reclaimed by Mumbaikers. Boats to Elephanta Island leave from nearby and the Gateway is thronged by Indian tourists and hawkers selling snacks, soft drinks, ice creams, toys, costume jewellery, magic tricks and giant balloons.

Just behind the Gateway is another of Mumbai's famous landmarks, the Taj Mahal Palace & Tower, commonly referred to as the Taj Mahal Hotel. This historic waterfront hotel is a Mumbai insti-

Going for gold at the Gateway of India

tution and many people still consider it the city's finest. Even if you can't afford to stay here, it's worth popping inside for a peek at the sumptuous interior and the magnificent central stairwell. The original entrance was on Mereweather Rd, but modern guests enter the old building from the harbour, passing under the huge central dome.

FIT FOR AN INDIAN!

The Taj Mahal Palace & Tower stands with Singapore's Raffles as one of the classic colonial hotels, so you might be surprised to learn that this grand building was built as a challenge to foreign prejudice. The founder of the Taj was the Parsi industrialist JN Tata, who embarked on this grand endeavour after being refused entry to one of Mumbai's British-owned hotels, allegedly for being 'a native'. Tata had the last laugh – the Taj is still going strong after more than a century, while the British hotels have faded into obscurity.

BOMBAY UNIVERSITY & HIGH COURT (4, C4, C5)

Set in a garden of breadfruit trees on the edge of the Oval Maidan, Bombay University is another grand colonial edifice. The university was designed in the 1870s by Gilbert Scott, who also designed London's St Pancras station. The centrepiece of the campus is the magnificent **library**, with its elegant Gothic arcades and fantasy staircases spiralling up each corner. Visitors are welcome, so wander upstairs for a look at the teak-lined reading room with its statues of long-forgotten university deans.

The library boasts the 80m-high **Rajabai Tower**, which resembles a Venetian church steeple fused with a minaret and topped by a Hindu *shikara* (temple tower). Under British rule the clock tower used to chime in the hour with 'Rule Britannia' and 'God Save the King/ Queen'. The base of the tower is ringed with statues representing the different ethnic groups of Maharashtra.

Next door is another of the city's grandest buildings, the Mumbai High Court. This bastion of bureaucracy is the highest court in Maharashtra and the courtrooms are packed out daily with lawyers, judges and plaintiffs. The elegant neo-Gothic building was constructed in 1878 and the **central tower** is topped by statues of Justice and Mercy – two elements frequently missing from the colonial justice system. The irony was not lost on the Indian stonemasons, who carved a one-eyed monkey tinkering with the scales of justice on one of the supporting pillars.

INFORMATION

- ☎ University 22673621, High Court 22677066
- ✉ Bhaurao Patil Marg, Fort
- $ free
- ☾ University 10am-7pm Mon-Sat, High Court 10.45am-2pm & 2.45-5pm Mon-Fri
- 🚉 Churchgate
- 🍴 court canteen on Eldon Rd

Pinnacle of learning, Bombay University

DON'T MISS

- The legal chatter of barristers outside the High Court
- Carvings on the Rajabai Tower
- Fine stained glass in the Bombay University Library
- Students playing cricket on the Oval Maidan

Visitors are welcome to wander around the compound and even sit in on public hearings, which feature some fantastically precise use of the English language. The public entrance is on Eldon Rd and the courtrooms are on the 2nd floor.

CHHATRAPATI SHIVAJI MAHARAJ MUSEUM (4, D6)

Housed in a magnificent Indo-Saracenic building on Mahatma Gandhi (MG) Rd, this is Mumbai's largest and most popular museum. Originally known as the Prince of Wales Museum, the building was built as a trib-

INFORMATION

☎ 22844484

🖥 www.bombaymuseum.org

✉ 159-161 MG Rd, Fort

💲 Indian/foreigner Rs 10/300,
   still/video camera Rs 30/300

🕑 10.15am-6pm Tue-Sun

ℹ free audio guide in Hindi, English,
   French, German & Japanese

🚉 Churchgate

🍴 museum snack bar

Cavorting in colour: a Mughal miniature

ute to the young George V (who was Prince of Wales at the time) by Scottish architect George Wittet, who also designed the Gateway of India. It's a chaotic jumble of onion domes, arches and carved balconies, topped by a massive dome styled after the Golgumbaz Mausoleum in Bijapur.

Inside you'll find one of the finest collections of Indian artefacts in the country, spread out over three sprawling floors. It's worth taking advantage of the free audio tour as not all the collection is labelled (you'll need to leave Rs 1000 or a piece of photo ID as a deposit).

Most of the ground floor is given over to a fabulous collection of **Hindu and Buddhist sculptures**, including ornately carved ceiling slabs from Aihole in Karnataka.

In the ground floor annexe is a small **natural history collection**, with a 6m-long sawfish that was hauled out of Back Bay in 1938.

The 1st floor houses the pride of the collection – a gallery of **Mughal miniatures**. Notable works include a portrait of Mughal leader Jehangir at Ajmer, illustrations from the Panchatantra (the Indian equivalent to Aesop's fables) and a delightful picture of two elephants cavorting in a pool.

At the top of the building, the 2nd floor houses a vast collection of Chinese and Japanese bric-a-brac and an impressive **gallery of arms and armour**. Keep an eye out for the personal armour of the emperor Akbar and steel 'tiger claws', chakras (razor-sharp Sikh throwing discs) and crescent-headed arrows, all designed to cut the throats of enemies! The last two rooms hold a fading collection of European paintings, including a Gainsborough and two Constables.

CHAKRAS

Chakras are commonly associated with yoga and meditation, but the chakra, or chakram, is also a razor-sharp throwing disc; the favoured weapon of Vishnu (the Sustainer), it is capable of dispatching an entire demon army. Using similar aerodynamics to the modern Aerobie, the chakra had a lethal range of more than 50m. Sikh soldiers carried chakras to battle right up until the 19th century. Few original chakras have survived but several are preserved in the Chhatrapati Shivaji Maharaj Museum.

MANI BHAVAN (3, B2)

This small but moving museum is housed in the building where Mahatma Gandhi stayed during his frequent visits to Mumbai. Many of Gandhi's core philosophies were conceived in a small room on the 2nd floor. The policy of satyagraha (literally, 'truth, nonviolence and self-sacrifice') was launched here in 1919, followed in 1932 by Gandhi's campaign of civil disobedience, which ultimately led to the collapse of British rule.

Inside, you can see a diverse collection of objects relating to the life of Gandhi, from photos and letters to the spartan room where Gandhi sat with his spinning wheel and contemplated the nature of existence. Although some exhibits are crumbling, it's a profound and affecting place and you can understand how the things said by Gandhi still resonate after more than half a century.

INFORMATION

- ☎ 23805864
- 🖳 www.gandhi_manibhavan.org
- ✉ 19 Laburnam Rd, Breach Candy
- $ free
- 🕙 9.30am-5.30pm
- ℹ free guide booklet in English, French, German, Russian & Hindi
- 🚇 Grant Road
- 🍴 several restaurants on Pandita Ramabhai Rd

DON'T MISS

- Gandhi's room
- Dioramas of Gandhi's life
- Photos of Gandhi's trip to London
- Gandhi's personal library

Gandhi memorabilia in Mani Bhavan

The lower level is taken up by **photographs and framed letters**, including a letter from Gandhi to Hitler calling for him to exercise restraint. British visitors will be interested to see the photographs of Gandhi's 1931 trip to London, where he famously suggested that British democracy would be 'a good idea'. On the 2nd floor are a series of miniature **dioramas** telling the story of Gandhi's life; you can also see the room where Gandhi stayed, with his writing desk, *charpoy* (rope bed) and spinning wheel.

The museum also has an extensive **library** of books and letters that were written by Gandhi and an **auditorium** where recordings of Gandhi's speeches are played on request. You can buy books and pamphlets written by Gandhi at the entrance to the museum. Renovations were underway at the time of writing, but were due for completion in late 2005.

NEHRU CENTRE & PLANETARIUM (3, B1)

Established in 1972 by Indira Gandhi, the Nehru Centre was conceived as a monument to national pride, secular values and scientific knowledge.

From the outside it looks like a conference centre, but inside is an innovative and thoroughly modern museum that explores the history and national identity of India, inspired by the writings of India's first prime minister, Jawaharlal Nehru.

The **Discovery of India** exhibition employs an impressive array of sculptures, audiovisual displays, photographs, cut-outs, dioramas, archaeological exhibits and model temples to tell the national story. It's an upbeat and inspiring exhibition and the displays may well persuade you to leave Mumbai and head out in search of the rest of India.

Some highlights of the museum include a section depicting the 5000-year-old Indus Valley civilisation, some reproductions of Buddhist cave temples and a mock-up of Fatehpur Sikri. There are also thought-provoking sections on colonial India and the freedom struggle. There is a great deal to see here and it's worth setting aside a few hours to properly explore all the galleries. In the same building is a small **art gallery** displaying work by contemporary Mumbai artists. The building itself is quite striking – it was designed by IM Kadri to reflect Nehru's vision of a modern secular India.

INFORMATION

- ☎ Nehru Centre 24964676, Planetarium 24920510
- 🖳 www.nehrucentremumbai.com
- ✉ Nehru Centre, Dr Annie Besant Rd, Worli
- 💲 Nehru Centre free, Planetarium adult/child Rs 35/20
- 🕙 10.30am-5pm; Planetarium closed Mon
- ℹ free guide booklet in English
- 🚇 Mahalaxmi
- 🍽 Jewel of India (p59)

The ivory tower of the Nehru Centre

Nearby is the popular Nehru Planetarium which attracts many bus loads of Indian students and schoolchildren. The programme varies through the year, but most shows include an intriguing mixture of astrology and astronomy. There are English-language shows at 3pm and Hindi shows at noon and 4.30pm.

DON'T MISS

- Colourful mock-ups of Hindu and Buddhist temples
- The walk-through model of Fatehpur Sikri
- Dioramas on colonial India
- Stellar shows at the Nehru Planetarium

DHOBI GHATS (3, C1)

If you've ever wondered what happens to your laundry after you hand it over to your hotel, head to Mahalaxmi train station. The station is surrounded by Mumbai's municipal dhobi ghat, where some 5000 dhobi-wallahs scrub and pummel the city's laundry. It may sound an unlikely tourist attraction, but the sight of thousands of washermen and washerwomen, soaking, scouring and beating the living daylights out of Mumbai's washing is certainly one of the most memorable images you'll take home from the city.

Mumbai's original dhobi ghats were located on the site of Victoria Terminus, but the British preferred to keep their dirty washing out of sight, so the dhobi-wallahs were shifted to the suburbs. Fortunately it's easy to get to the Mahalaxmi ghats – the causeway next to Mahalaxmi station offers a panoramic view over the whole area. If you've recently handed in any laundry at your hotel, it may well be down there somewhere among the tubs, troughs and washing lines.

If you fancy a closer look, follow the concrete steps down from the causeway. Officially, visitors are discouraged from the laundry compound, but enterprising launderers offer unofficial tours of the ghats for around Rs 100. Photography is prohibited inside the compound, but you may be permitted to take a few shots if a launderer is showing you around.

INFORMATION

- ✉ Dr E Moses Rd, Mahalaxmi
- 💲 free
- 🕑 4.30am-sunset
- 🚇 Mahalaxmi
- 🍴 Gallops (p61)

DHOBI MARKS

Laundry is an art form in India and dhobi-wallahs employ a secret system of 'dhobi marks' to identify the washing from individual addresses. Traditional dhobi marks were invisible to the untrained eye, but dhobi-wallahs are increasingly turning to indelible ink. Dhobi marks continue to play an important role in Indian forensics — many crimes are said to have been solved solely from the dhobi marks on victims' clothing.

HAJI ALI DARGAH (3, B1)

At the north end of Peddar Rd in Breach Candy, a narrow stone causeway leads out to Mumbai's most important Muslim shrine, the Haji Ali Dargah. The dargah was built in the 19th century as a mausoleum for the Muslim saint Haji Ali. According to one story, Haji Ali was a wealthy Mumbai businessman who renounced material possessions after a pilgrimage to Mecca and devoted the rest of his life to meditation on the shores of Back Bay. In another version, the saint died en route to Mecca and his body was thrown overboard with a message requesting that it be buried wherever it washed ashore.

Whatever the truth of the matter, thousands of pilgrims from all religions march along the wave-lashed causeway daily to pay their respects at the mausoleum, which is frequently obscured by a vast mound of devotional flags. Non-Muslims are welcome but photography is prohibited inside the compound and you must remove your shoes to enter the main shrine. Keep an ear out for devotional chanting from the pavilion beside the mausoleum.

The causeway to Haji Ali is lined with beggars, but the giving of alms is a pillar of Islam and making a donation is a well-organised business. Moneychangers are on hand to change your banknotes for coins so you can donate to every needy person. Note that Haji Ali is only accessible at low tide. The island is totally cut off from the mainland for several hours each day and the shrine gates are locked until the waters recede. If you do get stuck, there's nothing to do but sit and make yourself comfortable until the gates reopen.

INFORMATION

- ☎ 24924221
- ✉ off V Desai Chowk, Haji Ali
- $ free
- ◷ 5am-10pm, closed at high tide
- ◉ Mahalaxmi
- ✗ food stalls at the dargah

Pilgrims congregate at Haji Ali Dargah

JUST JUICE

On the roundabout by the start of the causeway to Haji Ali is Mumbai's most popular juice bar, the **Haji Ali Juice Centre** (V Desai Chowk; ◷ 5am-1.30am). This Mumbai institution has been refreshing pilgrims for decades, and the selection of sweet, savoury and even diabetic-friendly fruit and vegetable juices is the finest in the city. Juicers are on hand to liquidise everything from carrots to pomegranates – ask for a juice without ice if you're worried about stomach upsets.

SASSOON DOCKS (5, A6)

Hold your noses, another big Mumbai highlight is the huge and bustling fishing docks located at the south end of Colaba Causeway (Shahid Bhagat Singh Marg). Pongy it may be, but the sense of energy and human industry is unmatched anywhere else in the city, and this is the best place to observe indigenous Koli fishermen and fisherwomen going about their daily business.

The Sassoon Docks were constructed in 1875 by the Jewish entrepreneur, David Sassoon, who also built the historic Sassoon Library on MG Rd. The wharf was originally used to unload cotton, but with the decline of the Indian cotton industry, fishing became the main activity. Today the docks employ thousands, most them from the local Koli community.

INFORMATION

☎ 56565656
🖳 www.mumbaiporttrust.com
✉ Colaba Causeway, Colaba
💲 free
🕑 5am–sunset
🚊 Churchgate
✕ Kailash Parbat (p50)

KOLI CULTURE

The islands that make up Mumbai are the ancestral home of the Koli people, a fishing community that once plied the waters of the Konkan Coast as far south as Goa and Mangalore. Most district names in Mumbai are corruptions of Koli names, including Colaba (from Kolbhat), Apollo Bunder (from Palva Bunder) and Mumbai (from Mumbadevi). Traditional Koli culture is rapidly disappearing from Mumbai but you can still see large numbers of Koli fishermen and fisherwomen at Sassoon Docks, many in brightly coloured traditional dress.

Koli women at the Sassoon Docks

The frenzied activity starts at around 5am, when dozens of fishing boats arrive at the docks to unload catches of pomfret, mackerel, *rawas* (Indian salmon), kingfish, prawns and *bombil* (fish that are dried and deep fried to make the famous Bombay Duck). Waiting on the quayside is a vast and efficient workforce of Koli women, who process, pack and freeze the fish before sending it out to markets across Maharashtra.

Visitors are welcome to observe the mayhem, but don't expect porters to ask before pushing past you with baskets of slippery fish. Sadly, photography is prohibited without permission from the **Mumbai Port Trust** (☎ 56565656; mbpt@vsnl .com). If you need some fresh air after visiting the docks, head to the nearby **Mumbai Port Trust Botanical Garden** (3, C5) on WG Union Rd.

While in south Colaba, it's worth seeking out the Church of St John the Evangelist, also known as the **Afghan Church** (3, C6; p22), dedicated to British soldiers who died in the First Afghan War.

BOLLYWOOD OR BUST

In 1999 the British Broadcasting Corporation (BBC) held a poll for the Screen Star of the Millennium. To their surprise, the winner was not Marilyn Monroe or Tom Cruise but Indian superstar Amitabh Bachchan, the grey-bearded presenter of the Indian version of *Who Wants to Be a Millionaire* and veteran of more than 100 Bollywood films.

Ever since the first moving pictures were shown here in 1896, Mumbai has been film crazy. The Bollywood movie industry, based in the suburbs of north Mumbai, is the largest in the world, producing a staggering 1000 movies a year. The stars of Bollywood – people like Amitabh Bachchan, Shah Rukh Khan, Aishwarya Rai and Preity Zinta – are probably the most recognised human beings on the planet, adored by one-sixth of the world's population. Their faces are used to sell everything from Coke to politics – some temples even sell medallions with gods on one side and Bollywood stars on the other.

Bollywood films are famous for their set pieces, with extravagant song and dance routines and hundreds of extras. Actors generally mime the songs, but the voices behind them are stars in their own right and movie soundtracks form the backbone of the Indian music business. Plots typically involve family loyalties, love triangles, fights against injustice and escapes from the slums, but it's not unusual to see serious subjects such as the dispute over Kashmir given the full Bollywood treatment. Even if you don't speak Hindi, you can usually work out what is going on.

Until recently the behind-the-scenes world of Bollywood was off limits to ordinary mortals, but salvation has come in the form of **Bollywood Tourism** (☎ 26609909; www .bollywoodtourism), a private Bollywood tour run by senior figures from the movie establishment. The day-long tour starts with an interactive visit to a purpose-built set, where visitors learn about acting, stunts, dance routines, directing and editing, and is followed by a visit to a working Bollywood studio. The only sting is the cost – US$100/75 per adult/child. Alternatively, you can pay Rs 50 to watch the Bollywood magic on the nearest big screen.

For more on Bollywood, pick up the magazines *Stardust, Filmfare* and *Cineblitz*, available from all newsstands. If you fancy a walk-on part in a Bollywood film, loiter around the Gateway of India in Colaba. Casting directors regularly come here to recruit foreigners as extras – it's an interesting and unusual experience and you'll get Rs 500 or so for your trouble.

Box-office magic – Bollywood at the Regal Cinema (p66)

Sights & Activities

GALLERIES & MUSEUMS

Mumbai has some excellent and interesting museums and galleries. As well as the places below, see Chhatrapati Shivaji Maharaj Museum (p14) and Mani Bhavan (p15).

Ballard Bunder Gate
(4, F3)
The ornamental gateway to the Ballard Estate has been converted into a small museum about the history of the district. There are photographs of long-departed Mumbaikers, nautical knick-knacks and displays describing the construction of the Ballard Estate.
✉ Shoorji Vallabhdas Marg, Ballard Estate $ free ⏰ 9.30am-12.30pm & 1.30-7.30pm 🚇 CST

Collectors' Paradise
(5, B1)
This swish commercial gallery on Lansdowne Rd (Mahakavi Bhushan Marg) offers very upmarket Indian artworks, including occasional treasures by such luminaries as Jamini Roy. Unsurprisingly, prices are through the roof.

☎ 22832809 ✉ 17-19 Lansdowne Rd, Colaba $ free ⏰ 9.30am-8pm Mon-Sat 🚇 Churchgate

Dr Bhau Daji Lad Museum
(3, D1)
Following a massive renovation, this intriguing colonial-era museum should be restored to its original 1870s glory. Housed in a stately Victorian mansion, the museum has a vast collection of archaeological relics, fossils and memorabilia from the Raj. Next to the museum is the original elephant statue from Elephanta Island (p8).
☎ 23757943 ✉ Dr Babasaheb Ambedkar Rd, Byculla $ Rs 2/1, camera Rs 30 ⏰ 10.30am-4.30pm Thu-Tue 🚇 Byculla

Jehangir Art Gallery
(4, D5)
Founded by the Parsi philanthropist Sir Cowasji Jehangir, this huge modern art gallery displays work by leading Mumbai artists. There's always something interesting and all of it is for sale, providing you can afford the Rs 10,000-plus price tags. Samovar café (p54) and Natesan's antique shop (p44)

Ballard Bunder Gate

share the same building on Mahatma Gandhi (MG) Rd.
☎ 22843989 ✉ MG Rd, Fort $ free ⏰ 11am-7pm 🚇 Churchgate

Kamalnayan Bajaj Art Gallery
(4, A6)
Pet project of the Bajaj engineering corporation, this small commercial gallery opposite the CR-2 shopping centre exhibits an interesting selection of work by local artists, all of it for sale.
☎ 22023626 ✉ Bajaj Bhavan, Jamnalal Bajaj Marg, Nariman Point $ free ⏰ 11am-7pm 🚇 Churchgate

Museum Art Gallery
(4, D5)
Downstairs at the Max Mueller Bhavan (Goethe Institute) on K Dubash Marg (Rampart Row), this small commercial art space exhibits contemporary Mumbai art. All the work is for sale and the artists often give talks on their creations.
☎ 22844484 ✉ Max Mueller Bhavan, K Dubash Marg, Fort $ free ⏰ 11am-7pm 🚇 Churchgate

---

ART FOR SALE

Mumbai must be one of the only cities in the world where most of the art on public display is for sale. The lack of permanent art collections in Mumbai is an ongoing mystery – the only conventional art gallery in the city is the National Gallery of Modern Art and the art on display is similar to that found in the commercial galleries. On the plus side, this does mean you can take a bit of Mumbai home with you when you leave, assuming you can afford the high price tag charged by Mumbai art dealers.

National Gallery of Modern Art (4, D6)
A stylish building on MG Rd at the main roundabout between Colaba and Fort, this gallery shows an ever-changing collection of pictures – some classic, some forgettable – by Indian artists. The Guggenheim-like building is worth exploring. ☎ 22881969 ✉ MG Rd, Fort 💲 foreigner/Indian/child Rs 150/10/1 🕙 11am-6pm Tue-Sun 🚇 Churchgate

TEMPLES, MOSQUES & CHURCHES

Afghan Church (3, B6)
Near the southern end of Colaba Causeway (Shahid Bhagat Singh Marg) is a lonely reminder of the human cost of empire. The Church of St John the Evangelist was built to honour the British soldiers who died in the Afghan and Sind campaigns of 1838–43 and came to be known as the Afghan Church. Ask around for the verger if the church doors are locked. ☎ 22020420 ✉ Navy Nagar, Colaba 🕙 dawn-dusk 🚇 Churchgate

Babulnath Mandir (3, B3)
Named for a grove of babul (acacia) trees that once stood on Malabar Hill, this handsome mandir (temple) enshrines a massive lingam (phallic image of Shiva; the creator and destroyer). It's worth coming just for the relaxing atmosphere and sea breezes. Follow the steep track from Babulnath Rd or take the elevator (Rs 1).

☎ 23673602 ✉ Babulnath Rd, Chowpatty 🕙 6am-10pm 🚇 Grant Road, Charni Road

Banganga Tank (3, A3)
Reached via a flight of stone steps from Bal Gangadhar (BG) Kher Marg, Banganga Tank is a wonderfully serene spot. The ancient bathing tank is flanked on all sides by Hindu temples and it serves as the focal point for the Banganga Festival in January (p68). At other times the tank is used as a swimming pool by local children. ✉ BG Kher Marg, Malabar Hill 🕙 24hr 🚇 Charni Road

Basilica of Mount Mary (2, A3)
This neat grey and white church is the most important Christian place of worship in north Mumbai. Locals believe that the Virgin has miraculous powers of healing and stalls in front of the hilltop church sell wax effigies of body parts, which are left at the altar in the hope of miracle cures. A major festival is held here every September. ☎ 26423152 ✉ Mount Mary Rd, Bandra 🕙 6am-1pm & 2-8.30pm 🚇 Bandra

Church of St Andrew & St Columba (4, D6)
This classic neoclassical church was built in 1815 to cater to the Scottish community in British Bombay. The doors are usually locked but music and theatre performances are held here from November to January as part of the Kala Ghoda Festival (p68). ☎ 26423680 ✉ Shahid Bhagat Singh Marg, Fort 🚇 Churchgate

Pilgrims browse stalls outside Mumbadevi Mandir (opposite)

ZOROASTRIANISM

Mumbai is home to the world's largest surviving community of Zoroastrians, Parsis who fled here from Iran in the 10th century to escape religious persecution. Zoroastrianism is one of the oldest faiths in the world – 1500 years older than Christianity and 3500 years older than Scientology. Zoroastrians follow the teachings of the prophet Zoroaster and believe in a single divine deity, Ahura Mazda, who is worshipped in the form of fire at *agiaries* (fire temples) around Mumbai. You can identify *agiaries* by the figures of winged bulls outside but only Parsis are allowed to enter. Many tourists develop a ghoulish fascination with Parsi funeral rites (the dead are laid out in the open air to be consumed by vultures) but the process is hidden from view in the Towers of Silence on Malabar Hill.

Holy Name Cathedral (5, B1)

Part of the huge Roman Catholic bishopric that sprawls along Wodehouse Rd (Nathalal Parekh Marg), this handsome Goan-style cathedral is full of trompe l'oeil frescoes and gaudy paintings of the saints. It opened in 1905.
☎ 22020121 ✉ 19 Wodehouse Rd, Colaba ☾ 8.30am–5pm ☒ Churchgate

Iskcon Temple (2, A1)

If you visit Juhu, detour north to this shimmering marble Krishna temple. Inside are dioramas on the life of Swami Prabhupada, founder of the Hare Krishna movement, and a pilgrims' canteen serving tasty vegetarian food. Look for the lifelike wax statue of the Swami in the courtyard.
☎ 26200248 ✉ Juhu Church Rd, Juhu ☾ 4.30am–9pm ☒ Vile Parle

Jumma Masjid (3, D3)

One of Mumbai's oldest mosques, the stately Jumma Masjid was founded in 1770. The current building is a glorious collection of domes, arches and minarets and it bustles with life for the weekly Friday prayers. You're welcome to look from outside, but the prayer hall is reserved for Muslims.
☎ 23425453 ✉ 46 Janjikar St, Kalbadevi ☾ dawn–dusk ☒ Masjid

Kenesethe Eliyahoo Synagogue (4, D5)

Founded in 1884, this brilliant blue synagogue caters to Mumbai's dwindling Jewish population. The interior is a fabulous concoction of sky-blue pillars, stained glass and chandeliers. It's open to people of all faiths but only Jews can enter during Friday evening and Saturday morning prayers.
☎ 22831502 ✉ 55 Dr VB Gandhi Marg, Fort ☾ 10am–6pm ☒ Churchgate

Mahalaxmi Mandir (3, B1)

One of Mumbai's busiest and most popular mandirs, this seafront temple is sacred to Mahalaxmi, goddess of wealth. It forms the focal point of Mumbai's annual Navratri (Dussehra) celebrations (p68) and there's an orderly queuing system to observe the statue in the inner sanctum.
☎ 24824732 ✉ Bhulabhai Desai Marg, Breach Candy ☾ dawn–dusk ☒ Mahalaxmi

Malabar Hill Jain Mandir (3, B3)

Built in 1904, this glittering Jain mandir on BG Kher Marg is dedicated to Adinath, the first *tirthankar* (teacher-saint) of Jainism. It's a fabulously kitsch affair, with vivid murals telling the stories of the 24 *tirthankars*. Remove your shoes and all leather items before you enter.
☎ 23692727 ✉ BG Kher Marg, Malabar Hill ☾ dawn-dusk ☒ Charni Road

Mumbadevi Mandir (3, C3)

Sacred to Mumbadevi (the Koli mother-goddess), this is the shrine that gave Mumbai its name. The original mandir stood near Victoria

Bull statue at a Parsi *agiary*

Holy Name Cathedral (p23)

Terminus (Chhakrapati Shivaji; CST), but it was moved to its current location in the 18th century. Pilgrims queue to pay their respects and browse the market stalls selling offerings, ceremonial headgear and painted wooden pots for tikka powder.

✉ cnr Sheikh Memon St & Mumbadevi Rd, Kalbadevi ☼ dawn-dusk ☷ Masjid

Raudat Tahera Mausoleum (3, C3)
Hidden away in the alleys of Bhuleshwar is this hand-

some Muslim mausoleum, containing the tomb of Syedna Taher Saifuddin, leader of the local Bohra community. The entire text of the Quran is written on the walls in gold and gemstones and the monument attracts a steady stream of Muslim pilgrims.

✉ cnr Dhabu St & Dharamsi St, Bhindi Bazaar ☼ dawn-dusk ☷ Grant Road

St Thomas' Cathedral (4, D4)
Spectacularly restored in 2004, St Thomas' Cathedral fuses elements from Byzantine and British colonial architecture. The cathedral opened in 1718 and is full of ostentatious colonial memorials, including the mausoleum of Dr Thomas Carr, the first bishop of Mumbai.

☎ 22839783 ✉ 3 Veer Nariman Rd, Horniman Circle, Fort ☼ 7am-6pm ☷ Churchgate

CAVE TEMPLES

There are several interesting cave temples in the northern suburbs. To reach any of the following caves,

charter an autorickshaw from the relevant suburban train station.

Jogeshwari Caves (1, B1)
The oldest Hindu caves in India, these rock-cut shrines were hollowed out in the 5th century. Locals still use the Jogeshwari Caves as a temple and there are some impressive carvings here, but the site has become run down and the caves have been almost swallowed up by nearby housing developments.

✉ Jogeshwari Caves Rd, Jogeshwari ☼ dawn-dusk ☷ Jogeshwari

Mahakali (Kondivita) Caves (1, B1)
East of the Jogeshwari Caves, this small group of Buddhist caves stands on the edge of the Aarey Milk Colony. Although the surrounding area is very built up, the cave temples are preserved in a tidy compound and inside are Buddhist carvings and an ancient stupa.

✉ Mahakali Caves Rd, off JV Link Rd, Mulgaon ☼ dawn-dusk ☷ Jogeshwari

Mandapeshwar Caves (1, B1)
This small complex of Shaivite caves is conveniently close to Borivali station. Most of the 1500-year-old caves are plain, but one chamber contains a magnificent carving of Shiva as Nataraja (the cosmic dancer), dancing the divine dance that created the universe.

✉ off Laxman Mhatre Marg, Borivali ☼ dawn-dusk ☷ Borivali

PARKS & GARDENS

Hanging Gardens (3, B3)
Neatly laid out and meticulously maintained, these ornamental gardens (also called the Sir Pherozshah Mehta Gardens) on Bal Gangadhar (BG) Kher Marg are perched atop Mumbai's main reservoir on Malabar Hill. Locals come here to picnic in the shade of animal-shaped topiary and wooden gazebos. Hidden from view among the trees below the park are the Parsi Towers of Silence.
⊠ BG Kher Marg, Chowpatty
💲 free 🕙 5am-9pm
🚃 Charni Road

Horniman Circle (4, E4)
Laid out in 1869, these ornamental gardens are vaguely reminiscent of the Hyde Park set from the film *Mary Poppins*. An ornamental wrought iron fence encloses a circle of formal gardens, jungle trees and snoozing locals. This is one of the few colonial creations to keep its British-era name – Sir Benjamin Horniman was a British journalist who wrote in support of Indian Independence.
⊠ Veer Nariman Rd, Fort
💲 free 🕙 dawn-dusk
🚃 Churchgate

Kamala Nehru Park (3, B3)
Although hopelessly overgrown, these gardens offer fine views over Mumbai. Steps lead down through the park to Chowpatty Beach, passing several viewpoints.
⊠ BG Kher Marg, Chowpatty 💲 free 🕙 5am-9pm
🚃 Charni Road

Maharashtra Nature Park (2, B3)
Opposite the Dharavi bus station on Nayak Nagar Rd, this 15-hectare nature park is a peaceful spot to hunt for birds and butterflies. Created in partnership with the World Wildlife Foundation, it's a refreshing counterpoint to the surrounding slums.
⊠ Nayak Nagar Rd, Sion
💲 Rs 5 🕙 9.30am-7pm
🚃 Mahim

Veermata Jijabai Bhosale Udyan (3, D1)
Surrounding Bombay Zoo and covered by the same ticket, these shady gardens, also known as Victoria Gardens, are a popular picnic spot in the city. Look for the bronze statue of Edward VII astride a *kala ghoda* (black horse) – it originally stood on the corner of MG Rd and K Dubash Marg in Fort, giving the area its name. Under 12s get in free on Fridays.
☎ 23742162 ⊠ Dr Babasaheb Ambedkar Rd, Byculla
💲 Rs 5/2, over 65s free, still/video camera Rs 10/30
🕙 9am-6.30pm Thu-Tue
🚃 Byculla

A piece of Hyde Park in Mumbai – gateway to the British-era Horniman Circle

NOTABLE BUILDINGS & MONUMENTS

Army & Navy Building (4, D5)
This elegant colonial build-ing originally housed the British Army & Navy stores, a vast department store catering to the whims of the British ruling classes. Today it's the setting for a more modern shopping experi-ence, the Westside clothing store (p42).
✉ 148 MG Rd, Fort
🕙 10.30am-8.30pm
🚇 Churchgate

Asiatic Society Library & Town Hall (4, E4)
Dominating Horniman Circle, the former Town Hall looks a little like an American plantation house transplanted to India, with a broad stairway rising to a brilliant, white-columned façade. It now contains the Central Library and the members-only Asiatic Society Library. There are grand statues of colonial heroes in the foyers of both libraries.
☎ 26600956 ✉ Shahid Bhagat Singh Marg, Horniman Circle, Fort
🕙 10am-8pm Mon-Sat
🚇 Churchgate, CST

BB&CI Railway Headquarters Building (4, C4)
Directly opposite Churchgate station, the old headquarters of the Bombay, Baroda & Central Indian Railway is covered with railway motifs, onion domes and busts of esteemed colonial gentle-men. It was designed in 1899 by Frederick Stephens.
✉ Maharshi Karve Rd, Churchgate 🚇 Churchgate

Brihanmumbai Municipal Corporation Building (4, E2)
Testing the idea that you can get too much of a good thing, Frederick Stephens covered the Brihanmumbai Municipal Corporation build-ing in onion domes. It all looks vaguely out of propor-tion but there are some proud-looking griffons on the front porch. Victoria Terminus is just across the road.
✉ cnr Dr DN Rd & Mahapa-lika Marg, Fort 🚇 CST

Elphinstone College (4, D5)
As you walk along MG Rd, take a moment to examine the handsome gargoyles on this historic campus, which was built with a donation from Parsi industrialist Sir Cowasji Jehangir. There's a bust of him above the main

porch. Sadly, the college is no longer open to the public.
✉ 156 MG Rd, Fort
🚇 Churchgate

Flora Fountain (4, D4)
Probably the most risqué monument in Mumbai, this mock-Italian fountain was erected in 1869 in honour of Sir Bartle Frere, who created the modern layout of downtown Mumbai. It immediately caused a stir with its bare-breasted, nymphlike maidens. If you're coming from Colaba, continue north along Dr DN Rd for more dramatic colonial architecture.
✉ cnr MG & Dr DN Rds, Fort
🚇 Churchgate

GPO (4, F2)
Mumbai's fine General Post Office is a classic Indo-Saracenic construction from 1911, with a massive central dome copied from the Golgumbaz mausoleum in Bijapur. Architecturally the building was a stepping stone towards the grander Chhatrapati Shivaji Maharaj Museum (p14) on MG Rd.
✉ Walchand Hirachand Marg, Fort 🕙 10am-8pm Mon-Sat 🚇 CST

JN Petit Institute (4, D3)
Topped by crenulations and absurd numbers of fleurs de

RESTORING MUMBAI'S HERITAGE
The row of stately colonial buildings along Dr DN Rd in Fort was conceived as a continu-ous covered arcade where the denizens of British Bombay could promenade without the sun affecting their pale European complexions. Sadly, the years have not been kind to Dr DN Rd. However, hope is now at hand, courtesy of the Heritage Mile Association, a group of concerned citizens who are committed to returning the street to its original glory. Since 2001 restoration projects have started on half a dozen buildings, and the group now has its sights set on the Flora Fountain.

lys, the JN Petit Institute was built by wealthy members of the Parsi community in 1898. Today it houses the HSBC Bank. Step back to admire the window details and stained glass on the upper levels.
✉ 312 Dr DN Rd, Fort ⏰ 10am-4pm Mon-Fri, 10am-1pm Sat 🚊 CST

Mint House (4, F3)
Hidden away on the wharfside in the Ballard Estate, the Indian government's Mint House stands close to the spot where the East India Company minted its first rupee in 1672. The current Mint House was built in 1827 – you can visit with permission from the mint master.
☎ 22662555 ✉ Shoorji Vallabhdas Marg, Fort ⏰ by appointment 🚊 CST

New India Assurance Building (4, D4)
The New India Assurance Building is wonderfully Teutonic. The frontage is covered with bas-relief depicting human industry, and sword-wielding maidens stretch up to the heavens on either side of the doorway.
✉ 87 MG Rd, Fort 🚊 Churchgate

Oriental Building (4, D4)
On the corner of MG Rd and Dr DN Rd in Fort, the Oriental Building, which houses the American Express Bank, is a classic colonial-era office building. It's worth popping inside to see the original 19th-century interior, rescued from beneath a 1970s façade in 2001.
✉ cnr MG & Dr DN Rds, Fort ⏰ 10.30am-4.30pm

> ## KABATUR KHANAS
> Members of Mumbai's Jain community avoid causing harm to animals in all aspects of their lives, which extends to strict veganism. Kindness to animals is an integral part of the Jain philosophy and followers of the faith offer grain to pigeons as a form of prayer. You can see several *kabatur khanas* (Jain pigeon-feeding stations) around Mumbai – there's one on Chowpatty Beach, one on Bhuleshwar St in Bhuleshwar and another on Walchand Hirachand Marg in Fort.

Mon-Fri, 10.30am-1.30pm Sat 🚊 CST

Sassoon Library & Reading Room (4, D5)
Founded in 1847, this historic library was built with a donation from the Jewish entrepreneur David Sassoon. Only members are allowed to enter, but a Rs 100 visiting membership (valid for 45 days) will get you access to the delightfully fusty reading room. On your way in, have a look at the bust of the turbaned, bearded Sassoon above the doorway.
☎ 22843703 ✉ 152 MG Rd, Fort ⏰ 8am-9pm 🚊 Churchgate

Sir JJ School of Art (4, E1)
Founded in 1857 by a Parsi philanthropist, the Sir JJ School of Art is one of the oldest art schools in the country. Lockwood Kipling, who also designed the bas-relief carvings for the gateway of Crawford Market (p28), was at one time head of the metalwork faculty at the school and his son, Rudyard Kipling – yes, *that* Rudyard Kipling – was born here in 1865.
☎ 22620488 ✉ 78/3 Dr DN Rd, Fort 🚊 CST

Standard Chartered Bank (4, D3)
Lavishly decorated with cherubs and flowery scrollwork, the headquarters of the Standard Chartered Bank has been lovingly restored – as a result the building looks as grand today as it did when it first opened back in 1902. Above the façade you can see carvings representing Britain, Australia and China, as well as a coat of arms bearing an elephant with a palm, a horse in a winch, a sailing ship and Britannia.
✉ 23-25 MG Rd, Fort ⏰ 10.30am-4.30pm Mon-Fri, 10.30am-1.30pm Sat 🚊 Churchgate

Standard Chartered Bank

PEOPLE-WATCHING

The following places are good spots for soaking up the atmosphere of Mumbai and watching Mumbaikers going about their business.

Ballard Estate (4, F3)
Founded in 1914, this planned district of stone office buildings was designed by architect George Wittet, of Gateway of India fame. The whole estate stands on reclaimed land and most of the important offices in Mumbai were based here until the creation of Nariman Point. Today it's a smart and quiet area, full of offices of shipping magnates.
✉ Shahid Bhagat Singh Marg, Fort 🚉 CST

Chor Bazaar (3, C2)
Mumbai's sprawling 'Thieves' Market' has hundreds of tiny shops and street stalls where vendors sell antiques, bric-a-brac, salvaged electronics, motor parts and pretty much anything else with market value. This is where Mumbai's different religious groups are tightly pressed together, and it's a fascinating area, despite ongoing communal tensions. The main area of the bazaar is south of Grant Rd, on the alleys around Mutton St.
✉ Mutton St, Bhuleshwar 🚉 Grant Road

CRAWFORD MARKET

Also known as Mahatma Jyotiba Phule, **Crawford Market** (3, D3; cnr Dr DN & Lokmanya Tilak Rds, Fort; 🕙 11am-8pm Mon-Sat) is the largest municipal market in Mumbai. From the outside it looks more like a medieval fortress than a place to buy household goods, but inside you'll find market stalls selling everything from fresh fish and suitcases to scrubbing brushes and dried dates. The market was constructed in 1869 and the main gateway is decorated with bas-reliefs by Lockwood Kipling, father of Rudyard Kipling. The open area at the back of the market is set aside for bulk fruit-vendors – if you come in Alphonso mango season (May to July), you can buy India's tastiest mangoes by the crate.

Colaba Village & Market (5, A5)
Many of the Koli fishermen who work at Sassoon Docks (p19) live in the narrow alleys of Colaba village, east of Colaba Causeway at the south end of the tourist zone. It's a friendly, slightly ramshackle neighbourhood with a loud and lively street market (along Lala Nigam St) and a small shipyard where energetic children

Get your fill of the food groups inside Crawford Market

A giant leap for mankind in Colaba village (opposite)

perform daring leaps into the ocean.
✉ around Lala Nigam St, Colaba ◉ Churchgate

Juhu Beach (2, A1)
Juhu has something of a split personality – at one end of the beach are towering beachfront hotels charging hundreds of US dollars a night, while at the other is Juhu Public Beach, frequented by Mumbaikers from all backgrounds, from the high-rises to the slums. Even if you stay in one of the posh hotels, stroll south to the public beach to enjoy fresh coconut juice, *bhelpuri* (Mumbai-style salad), *gola* (crushed ice with fruit syrup) and hand-operated fairground rides.
✉ Juhu-Tara Rd, Juhu ◉ Vile Parle

Kotachiwadi (3, C3)
Crucifixes and Portuguese name plaques distinguish this small Christian enclave from the surrounding Hindu and Muslim neighbourhoods. The alleys around the junction of RR Roy Marg and Jagannath (J) Shankarsheth Marg are lined with quaint two-storey wooden houses,

the last remnants of the Christian *wadi* (hamlet) that stood here before the rise of Mumbai. It's a calm and peaceful place to wander around.
✉ cnr RR Roy & J Shankarsheth Margs, Girgaum ◉ Charni Road

Linking Road (2, A3)
Out with the old, in with the new – Linking Rd is the beating heart of Bandra's shopping district and the streets are thronged by merry gangs of shopaholics snapping up bargain shoes and designer brands. Nowhere else is the gap between rich and poor so apparent. Expect air-kisses, designer handbags and the constant ring of mobile phones.
✉ Linking Rd, Bandra ◉ Bandra

Malabar Hill (3, A3–B3)
Dominating the peninsula northwest of Chowpatty Beach, Malabar Hill is one of Mumbai's most exclusive addresses. Here you'll find towering sea-view apartment buildings and the odd palatial mansion belonging to one of the founding families of Mumbai. There

are numerous things to see on the hilltop, including the Hanging Gardens (p25) and the tranquil Banganga Tank (p22). Unfortunately, the Raj Bhavan (Government House) at the tip of the peninsula is off limits to visitors.
✉ around BG Kher Marg, Chowpatty ◉ Charni Road, Grant Road

Oval & Azad Maidans
(4, C1–C6)
The huge open area west of the High Court (p13) is all that remains of the seafront esplanade outside the walls of the British fort – all the land between Maharshi Karve Rd and the sea was reclaimed during the 1920s. Today the Oval and Azad Maidans provide a welcome patch of open space in the middle of Fort. Come here after lunch to watch locals playing cricket in the afternoon sunshine.
✉ Bhaurao Patil Marg, Fort ⏱ 6am-10pm ◉ Churchgate, CST

Crawford Market (opposite)

ACTIVITIES

Bowling Co (1, A2)
Both kids and adults will enjoy sending pins flying at this huge bowling alley in the Phoenix Mills Shopping Centre. There are eight lanes downstairs and four family lanes upstairs and the mood is boisterous. The entry fee includes shoe hire and there are bars, snack stands and kids' video games in the same compound.
☎ 24914000 ⌧ High Street Phoenix, 462 Senapati Bhapat Marg, Lower Parel $ Mon, Tue & Thu Rs 199, Sat & Sun Rs 244, Wed Rs 99, until 6pm Fri Rs 59, then Rs 199 ⏲ 11am-12.30am ⓡ Lower Parel

H_2O (3, B3)
During the dry season, you can indulge in an incredible variety of water sports on Chowpatty Beach. H_2O offers water-skiing, parasailing, jet-ski rides, kayak hire and windsurfing, as well as boat cruises round the bay (p37).

JOGGING IN MUMBAI
Hundreds of upwardly mobile Mumbaikers gather every morning on Marine Dr to engage in jogging and other physical jerks. The long run from Nariman Point (3, C4) to the top of Malabar Hill (3, B3) is an epic jogging route and you can admire fabulous views over Mumbai from Kamala Nehru Park while you catch your breath. Come early in the morning to beat the heat.

Drop into the stand at the south end of Chowpatty Beach to see if anything takes your fancy.
☎ 23677546 ⌧ Chowpatty Seaface, Chowpatty $ varies with the water sport ⏲ 10am-10pm, closed in monsoon ⓡ Charni Road

Horse-Carriage Rides (5, C2)
Every morning dozens of ornately decorated victorias (horse-drawn carriages) line up along the waterfront at Apollo Bunder offering scenic joyrides around Colaba. The hammered metal bodywork on the carriages is a sight to behold and the fresh breeze in your face can be wonderful

on a muggy monsoon afternoon. You'll need to arrange a route and fare directly with the driver.
⌧ Gateway of India, Apollo Bunder $ per 30min Rs 300 ⏲ 10am-10pm ⓡ Churchgate

MSLTA (5, A2)
Tennis players with their own rackets can take advantage of the excellent facilities at the Maharashtra State Lawn Tennis Association (MSLTA) complex. Courts should be booked in advance.
☎ 22874806 ⌨ www .mslta.org ⌧ 165 Maharshi Karve Rd, Colaba $ per hr Rs 150 ⏲ 7am-10am & 3-6.45pm ⓡ Churchgate

A horse sleepily awaits passengers at the Gateway of India

MUMBAI FOR CHILDREN

Mumbai is poorly set up for people travelling with children. Most top-end and deluxe hotels can arrange a babysitter, but if you are staying anywhere else, going out without your children is a tricky proposition. If you want to go out as a family, restaurants are generally welcoming and cinemas are an obvious choice. Another night-time option for families is the Bowling Co bowling alley in Phoenix Mills (opposite). See also Chowpatty Beach (p10) and H_2O (opposite), and for a bite, Dosa Diner (p56).

Admission for many children's attractions is based on height; entry is typically half-price for children from 91cm (3ft) to 1.2m (4ft) and free for children under 91cm.

EsselWorld (1, A1)
In case you were wondering what the sign on the back of all Mumbai cabs meant, EsselWorld is Mumbai's best and brightest theme park. There are more than 68 rides spread over 27.5 hectares; it's reached via a Rs 20 ferry ride from Marve jetty near Malad. You can also get here on tours from the Gateway of India.
☎ 28452222 🖳 www.esselworld.com ✉ Gorai Island, Borivali 💲 Rs 270/220, under 1m free 🕙 11am-7pm 🚇 Borivali

Fantasyland (1, B1)
The only theme park within the city limits, Fantasyland has a decent collection of thrill rides, including a looping roller coaster, a water coaster and a selection of gentler swing rides and merry-go-rounds. There are great views from the precarious-looking 'Sky Cycle'.
☎ 28365683 ✉ JV Link Rd, Jogeshwari 💲 Rs 199/150, under 91cm free 🕙 11am-8pm Tue-Sun 🚇 Jogeshwari

Mumbai Zoo (3, D1)
Set in wonderful sprawling gardens near the Dr Bhau Daji Lad Museum in Byculla, the Mumbai Zoo (Veermata Jijabai Bhosale Udyan) is a better experience than you might expect. Cages are a decent size and the animals – including tigers, elephants, bears and crocodiles – seem less stressed than at many Asian zoos. To preserve the clean environment, plastic bags and water bottles are banned. Under 12s get in free on Fridays.
☎ 23742162 ✉ Dr Babasaheb Ambedkar Rd, Byculla 💲 Rs 5/2, over 65s free, still/video camera Rs 10/30 🕙 9am-6.30pm Thu-Tue 🚇 Byculla

Nehru Science Centre (3, C1)
Behind the better known Nehru Centre, this 2.4-hectare learning zone has any number of buttons and levers to play with, so you can sneak some covert education under their radar. It also has gardens, peacocks and a gift shop selling science-related toys.
☎ 24932667 ✉ Dr E Moses Rd, Worli 💲 Rs 15/5 🕙 10.30am-6.30pm 🚇 Mahalaxmi

Suraj Water Park (1, B1)
Ride the suburban train to Thane to reach this all-swimming, all-splashing water park. There are more than 30 water-based games and rides, including a fabulous Shiva and Ganga water slide, and you can hire swimming costumes, goggles and caps.
☎ 25974747 ✉ Waghbil Naka, Ghodbunder Rd, Thane 💲 Rs 250/200, under 1.2m Rs 100, under 91cm free 🕙 10am-6pm 🚇 Thane

Taraporewala Aquarium (3, C3)
It may not be up to the standard of Sydney Aquarium, but this old-fashioned place still attracts bus loads of school kids. Inside you'll find reef fish, scary piranhas, a 'Quran fish' bearing the Arabic word for 'greatness of God' and some bored-looking sea turtles.
☎ 26551943 ✉ Marine Dr, Chowpatty 💲 Rs 15/10 🕙 10am-7pm Tue-Sun 🚇 Charni Road

Water Kingdom (1, A1)
With wave machines, a lazy river and more than 20 water slides, Water Kingdom is the largest water park in Asia. It's attached to the EsselWorld theme park in Borivali, and is reached by the same ferry.
☎ 28452222 🖳 www.esselworld.com/waterkingdom ✉ Gorai Island, Borivali 💲 Rs 290/240, under 1m free 🕙 11am-7pm 🚇 Borivali

Trips & Tours

WALKING TOURS
Footsteps of the Raj

Built on the foundations of the British fort, the area between the Gateway of India and Victoria Terminus (Chhatrapati Shivaji Terminus) contains some of Mumbai's finest colonial buildings. Start at the **Gateway of India** (**1**; p12) and visit the grand **Taj Mahal Palace & Tower** (**2**; p12). Next walk northwest along Chhatrapati Shivaji Marg, passing the Deco **Regal Cinema** (**3**; p66).

Stroll up Mahatma Gandhi (MG) Rd for some culture at the **National Gallery of Modern Art** (**4**; p22) or the **Chhatrapati Shivaji Maharaj Museum** (**5**; p14), before continuing past the ornate frontages of **Elphinstone College** (**6**; p26), the **Sassoon Library** (**7**; p27) and the **Army & Navy Building** (**8**; p26). Take a short hop southeast for the **restaurants** (**9**) on K Dubash Marg (Rampart Row).

Return to MG Rd and walk west down AS D'Mello Rd to the **Oval Maidan** (**10**; p29), then turn right along Bhaurao Patil Marg, passing **Bombay University** (**11**; p13) and the elegant **High Court** (**12**; p13). Walk back to MG Rd along Veer Nariman Rd, pausing to admire the **Flora Fountain** (**13**; p26). Note the ornate **Oriental Building** (**14**; p27) and **Standard Chartered Bank** (**15**; p27) as you walk north along MG Rd.

After around 200m turn right along Maharshi Dadhichi Marg, then left along Dr DN Rd by the **JN Petit Institute** (**16**; p26). Across the road, two winged bulls mark the entrance to the **Vatcha Parsi agiary** (**17**; p23). Finally, walk north along Dr DN Rd, passing more grand colonial arcades to finish at **Victoria Terminus** (**18**; p11), where taxis and trains wait to take you home.

The Taj Mahal Palace & Tower viewed through the Gateway of India

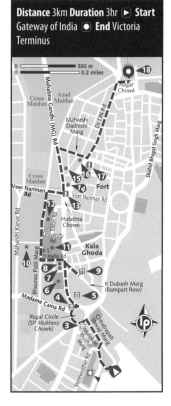

Distance 3km **Duration** 3hr ▶ **Start** Gateway of India ⬤ **End** Victoria Terminus

Mumbai Markets

Squeezed in between Lokmanya Tilak Rd and Grant Rd, Mumbai's sprawling market quarter is crammed with stalls selling everything from sequins and saris to toothpaste and tin boxes. Start off the journey at **Crawford Market** (**1**; p28) and investigate the wonderful **steel-pot shops** (**2**) on Lokmanya Tilak Rd.

Next walk up Sheikh Memon St for a tasty thali (traditional all-you-can-eat meal) at **Rajdhani** (**3**; p56) and stop for a peek at the eye-

Flower-vendor's display

catching **Jumma Masjid** (**4**; p23). Continue north along Sheikh Memon St to Mumbadevi Rd, ducking down the alley to see the atmospheric **Mumbadevi**

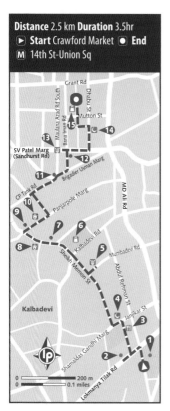

Distance 2.5 km **Duration** 3.5hr
▶ **Start** Crawford Market ● **End**
Ⓜ 14th St-Union Sq

Mandir (**5**; p23). Then cross the next junction to Bhuleshwar St, passing by the ancient **Bhuleshwar Market** (**6**; p43). Just north is a series of fragrant lanes packed with **flower vendors** (**7**) and a **kabatur khana** (**8**; Jain pigeon-feeding station).

Visit the **religious market** (**9**) and **Jain Mandir** (**10**) on Panjarpole Rd and turn left on Panjarpole First St, then right on CP Tank Rd to reach **Yadnik Chowk** (**11**), where plumbers and painters wait for customers on the roadside. Walk east along Brigadier Usman Marg and turn left into Bara Iman Rd, passing a bustling **wet & dry market** (**12**). Just west of the junction with SV Patel Marg (Sandhurst Rd) is a colourful **Shiv Mandir** (**13**; Shiva temple) – allegedly protected by supernatural snakes.

Next walk east along SV Patel Marg and turn left on Dhabu St to reach the stately **Raudat Tahera Mausoleum** (**14**; p24). Turn left at the next junction and then turn right and finish off in the **Mutton St Market** (**15**; p43). Finally, hail a taxi on Grant Rd to take you home.

The Queen's Necklace

Every morning and evening, hundreds of Mumbaikers promenade along Marine Dr (Netaji Subashchandra Bose Marg) – known as the Queen's Necklace for its curving sweep of street lights – to enjoy the cooling sea breezes from the bay. From Churchgate station head to the **Hilton Towers hotel** (**1**; p70), at the southern end of the drive in Nariman Point. Join the locals and stroll north, passing by a string of elegant Art Deco **apartment buildings** (**2**) – some of the most desirable real estate in India.

Dig in at Cream Centre (p56), Chowpatty Beach

When you reach Veer Nariman Rd, make a detour to **Mocha** (**3**; p54) for a coffee and a puff on a hookah, then continue north along the seafront.

You'll soon pass **Wankhede Stadium** (**4**; p67), which is the main venue for cricket in leather-and-willow-obsessed Mumbai. Beyond the stadium on Marine Dr are a string of private **gymkhanas** (**5**; sporting clubs) and the modest **Taraporewala Aquarium** (**6**; p31).

Continue to the start of the famous **Chowpatty Beach** (**7**; p10), where **H$_2$0** (**8**; p37) offers sea cruises, paragliding and windsurfing on the waters of Back Bay. Dry off with a leisurely stroll along the sand and refuel with a plate of tasty *bhelpuri* (Mumbai-style salad), or cross the road to the insanely popular **Cream Centre** (**9**; p56) restaurant.

From Chowpatty, follow the steps past the overgrown viewpoints of **Kamala Nehru Park** (**10**; p25) to the tidier **Hanging Gardens** (**11**; p25). Hidden from view in the forest below the park are Mumbai's **Towers of Silence** (**12**), where the Parsi community lay out their dead. OK, you're done – reward yourself with a cab ride back to your hotel!

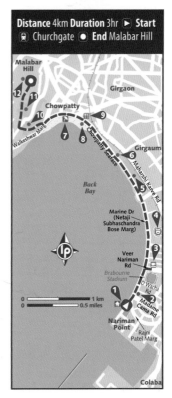

Distance 4km **Duration** 3hr ▶ **Start**
🚉 Churchgate ● **End** Malabar Hill

Malabar Hill

Girgaon

Chowpatty

Walkeshwar Marg

Girgaum

Mahurshi Karve Rd

Chowpatty Seaface

Back Bay

Marine Dr
(Netaji
Subhaschandra
Bose Marg)

Veer
Nariman
Rd

Brabourne
Stadium

To Wacha
Rd

Nariman
Point

Madame
Cama Rd

Rajni
Patel Marg

0 ——— 1 km
0 ——— 0.5 miles

Colaba

DAY TRIPS
Sanjay Gandhi National Park & Kanheri Caves (1, B1)

It's surprising how few Mumbaikers take advantage of this fantastic resource right on their doorstep – a 104-sq-km area of jungle teeming with wild birds, butterflies and rarely seen leopards. For now, Sanjay Gandhi National Park is a haven of peace and calm, but urban encroachment is nibbling away at the edges and growing numbers of squatter families are taking up residence on the park fringes.

Most visitors concentrate on the area near the park entrance (accessible by autorickshaw from Borivali station), which has a **boating lake**, a **nature interpretation centre** and the **Jungle & Tiger Safari** (adult/child Rs 30/15) – basically a bus tour with free-roaming lions and tigers.

INFORMATION
90 minutes by suburban train & taxi
- 🚆 Churchgate or CST train to Borivali (then taxi to Kanheri Caves)
- ☎ India Tourism 22074333
- 💲 2nd-/1st-class train Rs 10/104, return taxi Rs 300-400
- 🕢 7.30am-6pm Tue-Sun
- ℹ information booklet (Rs 15) available at caves
- 🍴 picnic or caves snack-stand

Altogether more interesting are the fabulous **Kanheri Caves** in the middle of the park, which are only accessible in an all-areas (single colour) taxi or in a private car. Although the carvings are less refined than those that can be seen on Elephanta, that's no great loss when you have 109 1st-century Buddhist rock-cut cave temples almost completely to yourself!

Allow a few hours to thoroughly explore the complex. Cave 3 is the most impressive, with an arcade of ornately carved columns surrounding an ancient stupa. Many other caves have Pali inscriptions and carvings of Buddha supported on a lotus flower – seek out Cave 2, Caves 89, 90 and 93, and the huge dining hall in Cave 11. On the hilltop behind the caves is a series of rock-cut tanks and plinths from long-vanished brick stupas.

The fascinating carvings at Kanheri Caves

Alibaug & Chaul

Alibaug is a sleepy beach resort that feels a million miles from the hustle and bustle of Mumbai. There are several clean, dark-sand beaches, a handful of beachfront cafés and a small cluster of *bhelpuri* and *gola* (fruit-syrup crushed ice) stalls plying tourists with drinks and snacks.

INFORMATION

90 minutes by boat & bus

- 🚢 Gateway of India ferry to Mandwa, then local bus to Alibaug
- ☎ Maldar Catamarans 22829695, India Tourism 22074333
- 💲 combined bus & ferry ticket Rs 70-100
- 🕑 ferries every 2hr, 8am-6pm
- 🍴 cafés at Alibaug Beach, Hotel Surabhi

Depending on the tide, you can wade or take a boat out to **Kolaba Fort**, the wave-battered Maratha fortress just off the main beach. There's another **Maratha fort** inland that doubles as the town prison. As well as the main **public beach** (a 15-minute walk from the bus stand), there are more secluded beaches at **Nargoan**, **Versoli** and **Kihim**, accessible by autorickshaw.

From Alibaug, a 30-minute bus or autorickshaw ride will take you to **Chaul**. On the outskirts of the village, in the direction of Murud, are some incredibly atmospheric Portuguese ruins, which spill out of the jungle onto the shore. Start your explorations where the massive fort walls cross the road, and stroll through the overgrown ruins of mansions and churches to an empty beach backed by whispering palms. If you're stuck waiting for a bus back to Alibaug, the nearby **Hotel Surabhi** serves cold drinks and Indian snacks.

Another interesting side trip from Alibaug is the 18th-century **Kanakeshwar temple**, reached via 750 stone steps from the road to Rewas, about 12km north of Alibaug. An autorickshaw will cost about Rs 300 return.

Boats to Alibaug stop running during the monsoon – to visit Alibaug out of season, your only option is the three-hour bus ride (Rs 61, hourly) from Mumbai Central Bus Station on J Boman Behram Marg.

Sunny skies at Chaul Beach

ORGANISED TOURS

As well as the following tours, taxi drivers by the Gateway of India (5, D2) run tours of popular downtown sights for Rs 550. However, these often include a visit to a pushy souvenir shop. Contact the Elephanta cruise booking desks by the Gateway of India for information on group bus tours and tours to Mumbai theme parks.

Bombay Natural History Society (4, D6)

Founded in 1883, the Natural History Society runs popular tours of unspoiled nature areas around Mumbai, including the Sanjay Gandhi National Park. Tours run every Saturday or Sunday, but you'll need to become a member to attend, which costs Rs 400 (valid for one year). Members cover their own transport costs.
☎ 22821811 🖳 www .bnhs.org ✉ Hornbill House, Shahid Bhagat Singh Marg, Fort 💲 Rs 10-20, plus membership Rs 400 🕓 10am-5.30pm Mon-Fri & 2nd/4th Sat

H₂0 (3, B3)

The water-sports centre at the south end of Chowpatty Beach offers short boat cruises around Back Bay for Rs 70 per person. Groups of six or more can enjoy longer harbour cruises (per person Rs 150) and night cruises (per person Rs 250) from 7pm.
☎ 23677546 ✉ Chow-patty Seaface, Chowpatty 🕓 10am-10pm, closed in monsoon

MUMBAI GUIDES

If you fancy more than the usual tourist spiel, hire an English-speaking guide from **India Tourism** (4, C3; ☎ 22074333; 2nd fl, Western Railway Reservations Office, Maharshi Karve Rd, Churchgate; 🕓 8.30am-6pm Mon-Fri, 8.30am-2pm Sat) near Churchgate station. Guides cost Rs 350/500 for a half/full day for up to five people and staff will help you plan a fulfilling itinerary. French, German, Spanish, Italian and Japanese-speaking guides can be arranged for an extra Rs 180.

The stately Asiatic Society Library & Town Hall (p26)

Heritage Walks

Run by two female archi-tects, these interesting tours explore the heritage of old Mumbai. Scheduled tours run monthly on Sundays (Rs 100), or tailored tours can be arranged for Rs 500 per person (for up to five people) – call or email for details.
☎ 26055756 🖳 heritage walks@hotmail.com

MTDC (5, D2)

Between the months of October and June, the Maharashtra Tourism Development Corporation (MTDC) operates a one-hour open-topped bus tour of the sights in downtown Mumbai. The tour includes the Gateway of India, Nariman Point, Churchgate, Victoria Terminus and Horni-man Circle. Tickets should be booked in advance at the MTDC booth located near the Gateway of India in Colaba.
☎ 22026713 ✉ MTDC Booth, Gateway of India, Apollo Bunder, Colaba 💲 upper/lower deck Rs 40/90 🕓 tours 7pm & 8.15pm Sat & Sun, no service in monsoon

Shopping

In recent years Mumbai has joined the ranks of Milan, Paris and New York as one of the world's premier shopping destinations. This is partly down to economics – prices are a fraction of those in most developed countries – but it also reflects a growing sophistication among Mumbai shopkeepers. You can still find the quaint government emporiums selling village-produced souvenirs and the chaotic, bustling markets, but these days you also have the option of shopping in air-conditioned malls and browsing the latest creations from internationally renowned Indian designers.

As a general rule, shops charge fixed prices but bargaining is the normal procedure at markets and street stalls. Most boutiques and emporiums accept international credit cards. Shops are normally open Monday to Saturday (see p84), but many tourist emporiums also open on Sunday. Sales are linked to religious festivals such as Diwali and Ganesh Chaturthi. If you buy more than you can carry, the post office has a reliable parcel service.

Mumbaikers love to shop, so you're in good company, but there are a few scams to watch out for. In particular, be wary of paying over the odds for so-called 'antiques' – many are fresh off the production line.

SHOPPING AREAS
Bandra Jewellery, shoes, department stores and pricey fashions.
Breach Candy Upmarket fashion boutiques and the occasional glitzy mall.
Colaba Souvenir emporiums, perfumes and brand-name fashions, plus a lively street market on Colaba Causeway.
Crawford Market & Chor Bazaar Antiques, temple goods, cut flowers, clothes, fruit and luggage.
Fort Pirated DVDs and software, electronics, government emporiums and Indian-style clothes.
Lower Parel Western brands and Indian designer fashions for sale in Phoenix Mills Shopping Centre..

EMPORIUMS

In Mumbai you'll find many fantastic government-run and private emporiums selling classic Indian souvenirs and handicrafts. Some examples include Kashmiri carpets, Indian pearls, carved elephants, papier-mâché boxes, pashmina shawls, brass Ganeshes, miniature paintings, sandalwood statues, inexpensive silver jewellery and marble models of the Taj Mahal.

EMPORIUM FEVER

If you get the emporium bug, there are state government emporiums dotted across the city. All sell state-specific arts and crafts and most have ongoing sales. Centrally located emporiums include the following, and there are more in the **World Trade Centre Arcade** (3, C5) on S Vaswani Marg near Cuffe Pde.

Rajasthan Government Emporium (4, D3; ☎ 20400502; 230 Dr DN Rd, Fort)

Kashmir Government Emporium (4, E4; ☎ 22663822; Sir P Mehta Rd, Fort)

Uttar Pradesh Government Emporium (4, E3; ☎ 22662702; Sir P Mehta Rd, Fort)

Kerala Government Emporium (4, A5; ☎ 22026817; Nirmal Bldg, Rajni Patel Marg, Nariman Point)

Bombay Store (4, D3)
A modern take on the old-fashioned emporium, Bombay Store has an excellent range of Indian arts and handicrafts, from incense and sandalwood to table lamps and T-shirts. However, you pay a premium for the stylish presentation.
☎ 22885048 🖳 www.thebombaystore.com ✉ Western India House, Sir P Mehta Rd, Fort ☷ 10.30am-7.30pm Mon-Sat, 10.30am-6.30pm Sun 🚇 Churchgate, CST

CCIE (5, C1)
A national institution, the Central Cottage Industries Emporium (CCIE) was established in 1948 to increase the profile of Indian arts and crafts. Prices are fair and the emporium has an incredible stock of Indian ornaments – make this place your first port of call.
☎ 22027537 🖳 www.cottageemporiumindia.com ✉ 34 Chhatrapati Shivaji Marg, Colaba ☷ 10am-7pm 🚇 Churchgate

CIE (5, B2)
The Cottage Industries Exposition (CIE), not to be confused with the government-run CCIE, is a private emporium on Colaba Causeway (Shahid Bhagat Singh Marg). It has overbearing sales staff but an impressive collection of Kashmiri carpets, brassware and Indian crafts. There's a branch on Juhu Church Rd in Juhu.
☎ 22818802 ✉ Colaba Causeway, Colaba ☷ 9.30am-8pm 🚇 Churchgate

Jamal Mir (5, C1)
On Lansdowne Rd (Mahakavi Bhushan Marg), this glossy Kashmiri emporium has a huge stock of Kashmiri carpets and *dhurries* (embroidered rugs). Staff can be pushy – take time to look through the silk and woollen offerings before you make a decision.
☎ 22020399 🖳 www.jamalmir.com ✉ Linden House, Lansdowne Rd, Colaba ☷ 9.30am-8.30pm 🚇 Churchgate

Khadi & Village Industries Emporium (4, D3)
Inspired by the teachings of Gandhi, this charitable emporium sells a huge range of handmade fabrics produced by rural communities from across India. As well as kurtas (long men's shirts), shawls and *salwar kameez* (a shirt, trousers and scarf for women), the emporium sells religious statues, brass knick-knacks and other Indian crafts.
☎ 22073280 ✉ 286 Dr DN Rd, Fort ☷ 10.30am-6.30pm 🚇 Churchgate, CST

Stop at the Khadi & Village Industries Emporium

BOUTIQUES

The following stores are excellent places to shop for high-end fashions. For workaday clothing and international brands, head to the **Fashion Street** (4, C3) clothing street market situated on Mahatma Gandhi (MG) Rd (near the Azad Maidan), Colaba Causeway in Colaba or any of the major department stores and malls that are dotted around town.

Chetana Craft Centre
(4, D5)

For a modern take on traditional Indian fabrics, head to this interesting craft centre–come-boutique, which is located around the corner from the Jehangir Art Gallery on K Dubash Marg (Rampart Row). The clothes, bags and accessories on offer here feature charmingly rustic colours and patterns.
☎ 22824983 🖳 www .chetana.com ✉ 34 K Dubash Marg, Fort 🕙 10.30am-7.30pm Mon-Sat 🚇 Churchgate

Courtyard (5, B4)

The Courtyard shopping arcade is housed in a historic colonial building. Here the work of more than 15 Indian fashion designers, including Ashish Soni and Narendra Kumar, is brought together in one place. Courtyard is situated on the waterfront in Colaba.
✉ SP Centre, 41-44 Minoo Desai Rd, Colaba 🕙 10.45pm-7.30pm 🚇 Churchgate

Ensemble (4, D5)

This gorgeous fashion boutique showcases six leading Indian designers, including Tarun Tahiliani, who created the dress for the wedding of Jemima and Imran Khan.
☎ 22872883 ✉ 130-132 Great Western Bldg, Shahid Bhagat Singh Marg, Fort 🕙 11am-7pm Mon-Sat 🚇 CST

Fab India (4, D5)

Arguably the best boutique in Mumbai, Fab India sells a range of shirts, trousers, kurtas and *salwar kameez*, all made from gloriously colourful block-printed silk and cotton. Orange, aquamarine and saffron are definitely the new black. Head upstairs for curtains and bed sheets in the same sunshine colours.

GET FITTED

Many items of traditional Indian clothing are one-size-fits-all, but Western-style clothing comes in the following sizes. Note that international brands are usually in European or American sizes.

Women's Clothing

India	S	M		L		XL
Aust/UK	8	10	12	14	16	18
Europe	36	38	40	42	44	46
Japan	5	7	9	11	13	15
USA	6	8	10	12	14	16

Women's Shoes

India/Aust/UK	5	6	7	8	9	10
Europe	35	36	37	38	39	40
France Only	35	36	38	39	40	42
Japan	22	23	24	25	26	27
USA	3.5	4.5	5.5	6.5	7.5	8.5

Men's Clothing

India/UK/USA	35	36	37	38	39	40
Aust	92	96	100	104	108	112
Europe	46	48	50	52	54	56
Japan	S	M	M		L	

Men's Shirts (Collar Sizes)

India/Aust/ Europe/Japan	38	39	40	41	42	43
UK/USA	15	15.5	16	16.5	17	17.5

Men's Shoes

India/Aust/UK	7	8	9	10	11	12
Europe	41	42	43	44.5	46	47
Japan	26	27	27.5	28	29	30
USA	7.5	8.5	9.5	10.5	11.5	12.5

Fabric at Fab India (opposite)

☎ 22626539 🖳 www
.fabindia.com ✉ 137 MG
Rd, Fort 🕑 10am-7.45pm
🚇 CST, Churchgate

Kala Niketan (4, B1)
It's worth going out of your
way for the impressive selection of saris at Kala Niketan.
Buying here is a friendly and
leisurely experience and the
staff manage to be persua-
sive without seeming pushy.
☎ 22005001 🖳 www
.kalaniketangroup.com
✉ 95 Maharshi Karve Rd,
Churchgate 🕑 9.30am-7pm
Mon-Sat 🚇 Churchgate

Kaysons (4, B4)
A megastore for shiny saris,
pashminas and silk scarves,
Kaysons has been dressing
fashion-conscious Mumbaikers for 20 years. There's
another branch in High Street
Phoenix (p42) in Lower Parel.
☎ 22843422 🖳 www
.kaysonsonline.com ✉ 4
Stadium House, Veer
Nariman Rd, Churchgate
🕑 11am-8pm Mon-Sat
🚇 Churchgate

Khubsons/Narisons
(5, B2)
This small shop on Colaba
Causeway sells colourful
T-shirts with a mixture of
inane and inspired mes-
sages, produced by the

successful Tantra T-Shirt
Company. Several market
stalls nearby sell similar tees.
☎ 22020614 ✉ 49 Colaba
Causeway, Colaba 🕑 10am-
8pm 🚇 Churchgate

Mélange (3, B2)
Fabulous clothes, fabulously
presented in a brick-lined
showroom near Kemp's Cor-
ner. Think sequined handbags
and jewel-draped *salwar
kameez* and you'll have some
idea what to expect.
☎ 23854492 🖳 www
.melangeworld.com ✉ 33
Altamount Rd, Breach Candy
🕑 10am-7pm Mon-Sat
🚇 Grant Road

TAILORS

Mumbai has dozens of tai-
lors who can knock up a
basic suit or ball gown for
a fraction of the price you
would find yourself paying
in Europe or the USA, but
when prices are this low,
why not spend a little more
and take home something
really refined?

Naina's (3, B2)
The couture house of Indian
designer Naina Shah,
Naina's sells off-the-rack
designer gear and extravagant made-to-measure

fashions, usually dripping
with sequins.
☎ 23613613 🖳 www
.nainashah.com ✉ Khatau
Mansion, 95 Bhulabhai
Desai Marg, Breach Candy
🕑 10am-8pm Mon-Sat
🚇 Grant Road

Reid & Taylor (4, D4)
One of several luxury suit
makers close to Horniman
Circle, Reid & Taylor can
turn out a magnificent
three-piece suit in 24 hours
with only one fitting. Prices
range from Rs 7000 for
lightweight cotton to Rs
20,000 for the best quality
woollen worsted.
☎ 22042630 ✉ 55A
Veer Nariman Rd, Fort
🕑 10.30am-7.30pm Mon-
Sat 🚇 CST, Churchgate

Telon (3, B2)
Men too often get a raw
deal when it comes to
designer fashions, but
Telon is working to restore
the balance. The Bollywood-
meets-Versace designs are
inspired. To achieve the full
Bollywood *masti* (fun) look,
pick up an embroidered
short kurta.
☎ 23648174 ✉ 149
Doctor Bldg, Bhulabhai
Desai Marg, Breach Candy
🕑 10.30am-8.30pm Mon-
Sat 🚇 Grant Road

FOOT FETISH
For the best in functional and fancy footwear, head to
the **Shoe Market** (2, C2) by the corner of Waterfield
Rd and Linking Rd in Bandra. You'll find dozens of stalls
selling leather boots, work shoes and slip-ons, glamor-
ous high heels, sequined slippers and beaded sandals.
If you're staying in south Mumbai, there are more
chappal (sandal) stalls in the street market on Colaba
Causeway.

DEPARTMENT STORES & SHOPPING CENTRES

Amarsons (2, C2)
An old-fashioned Indian department store, with costume jewellery, women's fashions and shelves of sparkling, sequined saris. Head upstairs for the womenswear section.
☎ 26418880 ☐ www .amarsons.com ✉ 269 Linking Rd, Bandra ◷ 11am-9pm ⊛ Bandra

Asiatic Department Store (4, B4)
Opposite Churchgate station, the Asiatic is the closest department store to Colaba, and sells a little bit of everything, from Indian fashions and beauty products to kids' toys and kitchenware. There's also an Internet café and a computerised fortune-telling machine.
☎ 22838179 ✉ Veer Nariman Rd, Churchgate ◷ 10am-8.30pm ⊛ Churchgate

CR-2 (4, A6)
Behind the Vidhan Bhawan in Nariman Point, Mumbai's newest mall is slowly filling up with expensive shops and fast-food franchises. Upstairs

is the glitzy Inox multiplex cinema (p66).
☎ 56548907 ✉ Rajni Patel Marg, Nariman Point ◷ 10am-10pm ⊛ Churchgate

Crossroads (3, B2)
Mumbai's biggest shopping mall, Crossroads is full of both Western and home-grown brands. As well as the boutiques, it has a kids' recreation area, a supermarket, a Chinese restaurant and the Piramyd department store.
☎ 23515890 ✉ 28 Tardeo Rd, Worli ◷ 10am-9pm ⊛ Mahalaxmi

Globus (2, C3)
Away from the main shopping zone at the south end of Waterfield Rd, this slick department store has plenty of designer clothes and an impressive selection of perfumes. If you tire of looking at brand-name clothes, there's a cinema on the top floor.
☎ 26436070 ✉ Hill Rd, Bandra ◷ 10.30am-10pm ⊛ Bandra

High Street Phoenix (1, A2)
Housed in a converted cotton mill near Lower Parel train station, High Street Phoenix has the largest selection of

import clothing in the city. Upstairs is Quorum, an arcade of designer stores with fashion by Krishna Mehta, Ritu Kumar and other Indian designers.
☎ 24943480 ✉ 462 Senapati Bapat Marg, Lower Parel ◷ 11am-9.30pm ⊛ Lower Parel

Shoppers' Stop (2, A3)
Shoppers' Stop is seven floors of fashions, fragrances, designer watches and jewellery in the heart of Bandra's main shopping district. Come here for the best range of brand-name perfumes in town.
☎ 26435424 ✉ Linking Rd, Bandra ◷ 11am-9pm Mon-Thu, 11am-10pm Fri-Sun ⊛ Bandra

Vama (3, B2)
Marked by a marble arch on Peddar Rd, this upmarket place is packed out with international brand-name clothes, from Reebok to Raymonds. Classy designs by the Indian designer JJ Valaya are showcased in the attached Valaya Studio.
☎ 23871450 ✉ 72 Peddar Rd, Breach Candy ◷ 10.30am-7.30pm ⊛ Grant Road

Westside (4, D5)
Another showy Tata enterprise, Westside targets the middle classes with affordable and functional streetwear. Upstairs you'll find a small selection of kitchenware and household goods.
☎ 56360499 ✉ Army & Navy Bldg, 148 MG Rd, Fort ◷ 10.30am-8.30pm ⊛ Churchgate, CST

STEEL-POT-WALLAHS
Along Lokmanya Tilak Rd in Kalbadevi you'll find dozens of **steel-pot emporiums**. These wonderful shops sell everything imaginable for the kitchen, from tiffin (snack) boxes and cook pots to teacups and rolling pins, all made from polished stainless steel. Pick up a copper-bottomed *kadai* (Indian-style wok) and kick-start your Indian-cooking career!

JEWELLERY

Modern Indian designer jewellery can hold its own on any catwalk, with elegant flourishes of silver, gold and platinum and delicate sprays of diamonds and pearls, but expect no subtlety from classical Indian jewellery. The fabulous Mughal-inspired creations drip with gold and gemstones – breathtaking but a little over the top for day-to-day wear. Indian pearls are particularly good value – the best prices are offered by the state-government emporiums (p39).

Popley Gold Plaza (2, C2)
With three floors of gold and diamonds, Popley is an Aladdin's cave of glittering gems. The refined modern creations will add sparkle to any little black number, but you'll probably need a whole new outfit to do justice to the traditional Mughal-inspired pieces.

☎ 26511349 ✉ 118A Turner Rd, Bandra ⏲ 10.30am-8.30pm ⊠ Bandra

Tanishq (4, B4)
The jewellery wing of the vast Tata organisation, Tanishq is famous for its distinguished designer jewellery, from whisper-thin bracelets to luxurious layered gold necklaces. Among other projects, Tanishq recently designed the jewellery for the Mughal-era Bollywood epic *Paheli*.

☎ 22821621 ✉ 7 Brabourne Stadium, Veer Nariman Rd, Churchgate ⏲ 11am-8pm ⊠ Churchgate

Tribhovandas Bhimji Zaveri (3, D3)
Tucked away in the alleys surrounding the Mumbadevi Mandir, Tribhovandas Bhimji Zaveri offers three floors of gold, gold and more gold. It's cheaper than some of the competition, but you'll still

Glamour galore, Popley Gold Plaza

pay a king's ransom for the more epic pieces.

☎ 23425001 🖳 www.tbztheoriginal.com ✉ 241/3 Sheikh Memon Rd, Kalbadevi ⏲ 11am-7.30pm Mon-Sat ⊠ Masjid

Vijay (3, B3)
Set back from the seafront in Chowpatty, Vijay specialises in heavy gold Mughal-style necklaces sparkling with rubies, diamonds and pearls. Bring your sunglasses and a well-stuffed wallet.

☎ 23639050 🖳 www.vijay-jewellers.com ✉ 67 Hughes Rd, Chowpatty ⏲ 11.15am-7.30pm Mon-Sat ⊠ Charni Road, Grant Road

MUMBAI MARKETS

With the rise of the shopping centres, attention has shifted away from Mumbai's markets, but there are still some interesting areas in which to browse.

Colaba Street Market (Colaba Causeway, Colaba) Mock antiques, T-shirts, knick-knacks and silk scarves (p28).

Crawford Market (3, D3; Dr DN Rd, Fort) Household goods, luggage, dried fruit and bulk mangoes (p28).

Fashion Street (4, C3; MG Rd, Fort) Discount casualwear, work shirts and baseball caps.

Fort Street Market (4, D3; Dr DN Rd, Fort) Electronics, pirated DVDs and software and (curiously) marital aids.

Kalbadevi & Bhuleshwar Markets (3, C3; Lokmanya Tilak Rd to SV Patel Marg, Kalbadevi & Bhuleshwar) Street markets in these districts sell everything under the sun, from flowers to temple statues.

Mangaldas Market (3, C3; Sheikh Memon St, Kalbadevi) Steel kitchenware, bulk fabric and cheap saris.

Mutton Street Market (3, C2; Mutton St, Nagpara) Rare antiques, among the junk.

Shoe Market (2, C2; Linking Rd, Bandra) Shoes of every shape and hue (p41).

ANTIQUES

Mumbai's antique shops are generally concentrated around the Taj Mahal Palace & Tower in Colaba, but prices are high and much of the stuff on offer is about as old as an iPod. Be particularly wary of 'antique' sextants, compasses, clocks, gramophones and brass wind instruments. Dedicated antique hunters may find some genuine articles among the ceiling lanterns and broken sunglasses at the **Mutton Street Market** (p43).

Ancestry (5, B4)
If you don't mind carrying a chandelier home in your hand luggage, Ancestry is full of ceramics and glassware, including some fabulously ostentatious Victorian lighting solutions.
☎ 22831358 ✉ Kamal Mansion, Arthur Bunder Rd, Colaba ⏲ 10am-7pm Mon-Sat 🚇 Churchgate

Framroz Sorabji Khan & Co (5, C1)
Near the Regal Cinema, this family-owned antique shop is full of interesting bits and bobs, including some gorgeous pieces of Victorian jewellery and old Mughal coins. You may be able to find some genuine treasures hidden away in the glass cabinets.
☎ 22021638 ✉ Chhatrapati Shivaji Marg, Colaba ⏲ 11am-6pm Mon-Sat 🚇 Churchgate

Natesan's (4, D5)
In the basement at the Jehangir Art Gallery, Natesan's offers rare items of furniture, brassware and religious art. You can't take stone antiques out of India, but the shop stocks original wooden temple-carvings that have been preapproved for export.
☎ 22852700 🖥 www .natesansantiqarts.com ✉ Jehangir Art Gallery, MG Rd, Fort ⏲ 10.30am-6.30pm 🚇 Churchgate

Phillips (5, B1)
Established way back in 1860, Phillips is a veritable treasure house of wooden carvings, Victoriana, brassware and 18th-century maps and prints. The antiques come with high price tags, but you can be confident that everything you may purchase here is the genuine article.
☎ 22020564 🖥 www .phillipsantiques.com ✉ SP Mukherji Chowk, Colaba ⏲ 10am-7pm Mon-Sat 🚇 Churchgate

Trafford House (4, D3)
For a mixture of antiques and modern furnishings made from antique materials, stroll around the display interiors at this upmarket emporium in the back streets near Victoria Terminus (Chhatrapati Shivaji Terminus; CST).
☎ 22090129 ✉ 6 Prescott Rd, Fort ⏲ 10.30am-7.30pm 🚇 Churchgate

BOOKS

Mumbai has a fantastic selection of bookshops and most of them sell imported novels and guidebooks as well as glossy coffee-table books on India and textbooks on Indian philosophy and culture. You can also find new and secondhand books at the roadside book market on the corner of MG Rd and Dr DN Rd in Fort.

Crossword (3, B2)
A huge air-conditioned 'palace to reading' with a vast stock of novels, glossy picture books, cookbooks, books for children, stationery, CDs and DVDs. There's a pricey café on the 2nd floor.
☎ 23842001 🖥 www .crosswordbookstores.com ✉ Sitaram Patkar Marg, Kemp's Corner, Breach Candy ⏲ 10am-9pm 🚇 Grant Road

Antique treasures at Phillips

READING MUMBAI

If there's one book that everyone is talking about, it's *Maximum City* by Suketu Mehta, an exhilarating account of Mumbai, told through the eyes of its inhabitants. Other novels with a personal perspective on Mumbai include *The Ground Beneath Her Feet* and *The Moor's Last Sigh* by Salman Rushdie, who grew up in Breach Candy. Rohinton Mistry described the Parsi experience in his novel *Family Matters,* while Anita Desai wrote about Jewish life here in *Baumgartner's Bombay*. Other Mumbai novels to look out for include *Love and Longing in Bombay* by Vikram Chandra, *Bombay Ice* by Leslie Forbes and *Shantaram* by Gregory David Roberts.

Magna Book Gallery
(4, D5)
Up an easy-to-miss stairway on the corner of MG Rd and K Dubash Marg, this well-stocked bookshop publishes its own books. Inside, you'll find a scholarly selection of titles on Indian culture and history.
☎ 22671763 ☐ www.magnabookgallery.com ✉ 2nd flr, 143 MG Rd, Fort ☼ 10am-8pm ⓡ Churchgate

Nalanda (5,C2)
In the posh Taj hotel shopping arcade, Nalanda has a respectable stock of picture books, postcards and imported novels and magazines, as well as home-grown Indian literature.
☎ 22022514 ✉ Taj Mahal Palace & Tower, Apollo Bunder, Colaba ☼ 8am-midnight ⓡ Churchgate

Oxford Bookshop (4, C5)
A Western-style book superstore, Oxford has two floors of books, magazines and music. The 2nd-floor café is a popular hang-out for students from Bombay University.
☎ 56364477 ☐ www.oxfordbookstore.com

✉ 3 D Wacha Rd, Churchgate ☼ 10am-10pm ⓡ Churchgate

Ritika (3, C4)
The bookshop at the Oberoi hotel has an impressive collection of imported novels and glossy picture books about India. It also sells international editions of European newspapers.
☎ 22843761 ✉ Oberoi Hotel, Marine Dr, Nariman Point ☼ 9.30am-10pm ⓡ Churchgate

SPECIALIST STORES

Bombay Paperie (4, D5)
Opposite the Bombay Stock Exchange, this unusual paper shop sells reams of hand-made paper, either loose for wrapping or made up into greetings cards, ornaments and delicate lamp-shades.
☎ 56358171 ☐ www.bombaypaperie.com ✉ 59 Bombay Samachar Marg, Fort ☼ 10.30am-6pm ⓡ Churchgate, CST

Cheemo (3, C4)
You can barely lift some of Cheemo's handbags for the weight of sequins and spangles. There's a branch

in the High Street Phoenix shopping centre (1, A2) in Lower Parel.
☎ 22853497 ✉ Oberoi Shopping Centre, Oberoi, Marine Dr, Nariman Point ☼ 10am-8pm Mon-Sat, 10am-6pm Sun ⓡ Churchgate

Chimanlals (4, D3)
Our favourite shop in Mumbai, Chimanlals is stacked from floor to ceiling with writing paper, envelopes, greetings cards, gift boxes and wrapping paper, all decorated with colourful Mughal and Hindu motifs. Enter from Wallace St.
☎ 22077717 ☐ www.chimanlals.com ✉ 210 Dr DN Rd ☼ 9.30am-6pm Mon-Fri, 9.30am-5.30pm Sat ⓡ CST

Handmade paper, Chimanlals

Mohanlal S Mithaiwala
(3, D3)
Mumbai isn't as famous for its sweets as Kolkata, but you can find some fantastic looking and tasting halwa (fruit fudge) at this *mithaiwala* (sweet shop) in the markets north of Crawford Market.
☎ 23439944 ✉ 271/3 Sheikh Memon St, Kalbadevi ◷ 9am-9pm Mon-Sat
🚇 Masjid

MUSIC

Indian pop and Bollywood movie soundtracks are the preferred choice of most local shoppers, but you can find a huge range of Indian classical music, as well as Indian classical instruments, at the following stores. If you can't find what you're looking for here, try the music sections at the Oxford (p45) and Crossword (p44) bookshops.

LM Furtado & Co (3, C3)
The largest and best of Mumbai's musical-instrument shops, Furtado's is stacked with fiddles, guitars, drums and sitars. Tabla sets with two drums, padded rings and a tuning hammer cost Rs 2350, while sitars start at Rs 2400.
☎ 22013163 🖳 www .furtadosmusic.com ✉ 540/4 Kalbadevi Rd, Kalbadevi ◷ 10am-8pm Mon-Sat 🚇 CST, Masjid

Planet M (4, E1)
In the Times of India building on Dr DN Rd, Planet M is Mumbai's leading music shop. It's packed with movie soundtracks, DVDs of Bollywood blockbusters and imported CDs of Western pop. You can listen before you buy.
☎ 56353874 ✉ Times of India Bldg, Dr DN Rd, Fort ◷ 11am-9pm Mon-Sat, noon-8pm Sun 🚇 CST

Rhythm House (4, D5)
An excellent choice for modern and classical Indian music, Rhythm House has racks of CDs and DVDs. Look out for the boxed sets of music by virtuoso performers such as Ravi Shankar and Nusrat Fateh Ali Khan.
☎ 22842835 🖳 www .rhythmhouseindia.com ✉ 40 K Dubash Marg, Fort ◷ 10am-8.30pm Mon-Sat, 11am-8.30pm Sun 🚇 Churchgate

PERFUME

The perfume trade in Mumbai is centred on Colaba. Some scents can be a little potent for Western noses, but generations of travellers have succumbed to the appeal of jasmine, sandalwood and patchouli oil. For more orthodox fragrances, brand-name perfumes are available at discount prices at many of Mumbai's department stores.

Ajmal Perfumes (5, B1)
A smart modern attar house near the Regal Cinema, Ajmal sells the full range of attars (essential oils made from flowers), as well as upmarket leather handbags, belts and wallets. There's a second branch (5, B4) on Arthur Bunder Rd.
☎ 22044077 ✉ Lansdowne Rd, Colaba ◷ 10.30am-9pm 🚇 Churchgate

Attar Ahmed Dawood
(5, C1)
This old-fashioned perfumer sells attars from gorgeous cut-glass perfume bottles. By default, perfumes come in plain glass, but you can upgrade to some fabulously over-the-top fragrance containers.
☎ 22870435 ✉ 6 Lansdowne Rd, Colaba ◷ 10.30am-8.30pm Mon-Sat, noon-6pm Sun 🚇 Churchgate

ESSENTIAL OILS
Perfume has been manufactured in India since at least 2000 BC but the industry really took off during the Mughal era, when India became the primary source of attars (essential oils made from flowers) for the Arab world. Dealers from the Persian Gulf still flock to Mumbai in huge numbers to stock up on essential oils – the most desirable attar of all is agarwood or *oud*, a sweet-smelling oil extracted from the bark of aquilaria trees that have been infected by a rare fungus. If you thought Chanel was expensive, a 10ml vial of agarwood essence costs upwards of Rs 3000 – by that reckoning, a standard duty-free-sized bottle would set you back US$500!

Inshallah Masallah

(5, B2)
Ask the helpful staff at Inshallah Masallah to guide you through the world of essential oils. Big sellers include lemongrass, jasmine, sandalwood and agarwood. Find it across the road from Electric House.
☎ 22049495 ✉ Best Marg, Colaba ⏰ 10.30am-9pm 🚇 Churchgate

HAIR & BEAUTY

Pampering aplenty: beauty products at the Taj Salon

Mumbai's luxury spas mainly cater to women, but men have their own unique beauty experience – the great Indian shave (see below).

Kaya Skin Clinic (4, D5)

If you feel you deserve it, Kaya Skin Clinic offers the works, from dermabrasion to Botox. Everything focuses on making the skin look beautiful, but this level of self-improvement comes with a hefty price tag.
☎ 56350921 🖥 www .kayaskinclinic.com ✉ 14 K Dubash Marg, Fort ⏰ 10.30am-8pm 🚇 Churchgate

Lakmé Beauty Salon

(4, B4)
Part of an India-wide chain, Lakmé offers very professional pampering and a wide range of skin and beauty

treatments to make sure you walk out glowing. There's a branch on Juhu-Tara Rd (2, A2) in Juhu.
☎ 22821255 🖥 www.lak meindia.com ✉ J Tata Rd, Churchgate ⏰ 9am-7pm Mon-Sat 🚇 Churchgate

Leela Health Club (2, B1)

The exclusive health club at the Leela Kempinski hotel offers the ultimate in spa treatments for those with deep wallets. Come for rubs, wraps and immersions, and leave looking like a million dollars.
☎ 56911234 ✉ Leela Kempinski, Sahar Airport Rd, Sahar ⏰ 6.30am-11pm 🚇 Andheri, Vile Parle

Taj Salon (5, C2)

Those who can, get their hair cut at the Taj. In the basement at the Taj Mahal Palace

& Tower, the salon offers threading, waxing, styling, make-up, nail care, henna tattoos and a full range of indulgent massages and reflexology.
☎ 22883934 ✉ Taj Mahal Palace & Tower, Apollo Bunder, Colaba ⏰ 9am-7pm Mon-Sat, 9.30am-5.30pm Sun 🚇 Churchgate

Touch of Joy (5, B3)

For a make-over with an extra degree of pampering, Touch of Joy offers relaxing facial massages with Ayurvedic herbal oils (women only), plus a full range of hair-care services, manicures and waxings.
☎ 22875993 ✉ JA Allana Marg, Colaba ⏰ 10.30am-7.30pm 🚇 Churchgate

Wellness Centre (2, B1)

Probably Mumbai's finest spa, the Wellness Centre at the ITC Grand Maratha Sheraton is a monument to indulgence. Make a day of it and finish with a splash in the pool and dinner at Pan-Asian, Dakshin or Peshawri (p59).
☎ 28303030 ✉ ITC Grand Maratha Sheraton, Sahar Airport Rd, Sahar ⏰ 6am-11pm 🚇 Andheri, Vile Parle

---

THE GREAT INDIAN SHAVE

Not all of Mumbai's beauty treatments are for women. Men can enjoy a traditional Indian shave, the full barbershop treatment with a cut-throat razor, hogs' hair brush, aftershave and a vigorous head and face massage. It costs just a few rupees and most barbers around Mumbai can oblige, but you should always demand a fresh razor blade.

Eating

Mumbaikers love to eat and the streets of the city are lined with an incredible variety of restaurants, cafés and snack stands. There is a huge gap between rich and poor, but street vendors at Chowpatty, Juhu and Nariman Point cross the divide, serving cheap, cheerful snacks to office workers and rickshaw-wallahs alike. At the other end of the scale are ostentatious luxury restaurants, where a meal can cost as much as many Mumbaikers earn in a month. In between are hundreds of relaxed cafés and family restaurants, which offer moderate prices and – usually – the option of air-conditioning.

The most popular eats in Mumbai are North Indian kebabs and curries, Mangalorean seafood and Chinese rice and noodles, but many places also serve interpretations of Western cuisine, which vary from the unconvincing to the sublime. You can also find Parsi food from Iran and dishes from the indigenous Koli people of Mumbai. Probably the fastest meal in Mumbai is the ubiquitous thali – an all-you-can-eat plate meal with a selection of curries and side dishes served with rice or chapatis (unleavened Indian bread). Vegetarians are catered for in almost all Mumbai restaurants.

Bookings are only accepted at top-end places but many midrange restaurants have bars where you can wait for a table. Tipping is optional (but welcome) and more expensive restaurants add 4% to 10% tax onto the bill. All but the cheapest restaurants have menus in English.

Hygiene is a concern for many foreigners, but you should be safe if you stick to busy restaurants and street stalls where the food is prepared freshly in front of you. It also helps to wash your hands before you eat – most restaurants have a washbasin for the purpose. For more information on Mumbai restaurants, pick up the *Times Food Guide* (Rs 150) from any bookshop.

Perk up at Barista (opposite)

COLABA

Colaba is the most popular place to stay and eat, with dozens of respectable eateries. Don't be afraid to try some the cheaper *dhabas* (snack restaurants) – many of these places serve excellent and hygienic food!

Bademiya (5, C1)
North Indian $
Every evening tables are set up along a narrow road near the Taj Mahal Palace & Tower and dozens of diners materialise from nowhere to feast on some of Mumbai's finest *seekh* kebabs (spiced minced lamb) and tandoori chicken. Find an empty table and soon enough a waiter will find you.
☎ 22848038 ⊠ Tulloch Rd 🕑 7-11pm 🚇 Churchgate

Barista (5, B1)
Café $
Easily Colaba's most popular café, this slick chain coffee house next to the Regal Cinema on Colaba Causeway (Shahid Bhagat Singh Marg) serves perky cappuccinos, English-style tea and an incredible array of cold coffee smoothies. There are branches all over the city, including Juhu (2, A1), Bandra (2, C2) and Fort (4, D2).
☎ 56336835 ⊠ Colaba Causeway 🕑 8.30am-1.30am 🚇 Churchgate

Bollywood Dhaba (5, C2)
North Indian $$$
As you might expect, the theme here is Bollywood and the entire interior of the restaurant is covered with old movie posters. The Mughlai food is good but a little expensive for the modest portions – try the *murgh murchi* (chicken) kebab with peppercorns and yoghurt.
☎ 56331555 ⊠ Mandlik Rd 🕑 11am-3.20pm & 7pm-midnight 🚇 Churchgate

Café Basilico (5, B4)
Italian $$
A relative newcomer in Colaba, Café Basilico serves fork-twizzlingly good pasta and gourmet sandwiches in a smart wooden dining room. All the bread is home-baked.
☎ 56345670 🖳 www .cafebasilico.com ⊠ Sentinel House, Arthur Bunder Rd 🕑 7.30am-1.30am 🚇 Churchgate

Cafe Churchill (5, A1)
European $$
Tiny Cafe Churchill, opposite Cusrow Baug, serves an impressive range of European-inspired dishes, including tasty prawn-and-pomfret lasagne and Irish stew. There are just a few tables so come early to beat the lunchtime rush.
☎ 22844689 ⊠ opposite Cusrow Baug, Colaba Causeway 🕑 11am-midnight 🚇 Churchgate

Cafe Mondegar (5, B1)
Café $
Café by day, bar by night, Mondy's is very popular with international visitors. The interior has buckets of 1950s charm – largely a result of the cartoon mural by Goan cartoonist Mario Miranda. The food is decent and the beers cold.
☎ 22020591 ⊠ 5A Colaba Causeway 🕑 8am-12.30pm 🚇 Churchgate

Delhi Darbar (5, B1)
North Indian $$
A friendly and unpretentious family restaurant with a solid menu of meaty Mughlai dishes. Order a half tandoori chicken, a plain naan and a salt lime soda and escape from the hectic bustle of Colaba Causeway.
☎ 22020235 ⊠ Holland House, Colaba Causeway 🕑 11.30am-midnight 🚇 Churchgate

Food Inn (5, B2)
North Indian $
Although it serves a bit of everything, it's the nonveg Mughlai food that stands out here. Take your pick of the chicken and mutton curries and order a creamy curd on the side to soak up the heat.

MUMBAI STREET FOOD
Street food isn't as popular in Mumbai as in many Indian cities, but there are still some excellent places to pick up a *channa puri* (puffed bread with chickpeas), veg sandwich or dosa (lentil-flour pancake) on the run. By far the best spot for street food is Nariman Point. At lunchtime thousands of office workers congregate at the street stalls on J Bajaj Marg and Free Press Journal Marg to munch on cheap, quick snacks, washed down with fresh lime sodas and gallons of sweet chai.

☎ 22042757 ✉ 61A Rabro House, Colaba Causeway ◷ 9.30am-midnight ® Churchgate

Golden Dragon (5, C2)
Chinese $$$$
Fabulously ostentatious, the grand Chinese restaurant at the Taj is all dark wood and ornamental screens. Dishes run the gamut from sweet-and-sour pomfret to beggars' chicken – a whole chicken cooked inside lotus leaves (24-hours' notice required).
☎ 56653366 ✉ Taj Mahal Palace & Tower, Apollo Bunder ◷ noon-2.45pm & 7-11.45pm ® Churchgate

Henry Tham (5, C1)
Chinese $$$$
You might feel like the Incredible Shrinking Man in the giant red velour chairs at this stylish Singapore-Chinese restaurant. Food is Straits Chinese with a modern twist and the flavours are sublime, but the dining room can seem a bit empty on weekdays.
☎ 22023186 ✉ Dhanraj Mahal, Chhatrapati Shivaji Marg ◷ 7pm-midnight ® Churchgate

Indigo (5, B2)
European $$$$
Mumbai's best European restaurant, Indigo serves intoxicatingly good European food in stylish surroundings, backed up by a global wine list. Few places in town can match the food, ambience and service – Bill Clinton ate here and loved it.
☎ 56368980 ✉ 4 Mandlik Rd ◷ noon-3pm & 7.30pm-midnight ® Churchgate

FLASH PAAN

For the perfect end to any Indian meal, pick up a sweet *paan*. This mildly intoxicating combination of crushed areca nut, sweet chutney, lime paste, rose petals and spices, all wrapped in a betel leaf, is a traditional aid to digestion. Mumbaikers like their *paan* coated in silver leaf and sprinkled with coconut. Look out for the *paan*-wallahs outside Mumbai restaurants such as Delhi Darbar (p49), the Majestic Hotel (opposite) and Indian Summer (p54).

Kailash Parbat (5, B2)
Indian Dhaba $
Many Mumbaikers fondly remember this place from their childhood and the food is as good as it has always been. The menu is dominated by pure veg dishes from Sind and you can soak up the curries with rice, *puri* (puffed fried bread) and naan.
☎ 22046079 ✉ 1st Pasta Lane ◷ 8am-11pm ® Churchgate

Kamat Restaurant (5, B2)
South Indian $
If the Colaba street market gets too much, duck into this simple split-level veg dhaba opposite Electric House for dosas (lentil-flour pancakes), *idli* (fermented rice cakes), *vada* (fried salty, savoury doughnuts) and the cheap-as-chickpeas house thali. Head upstairs for icy air-con.
☎ 22874734 ✉ Colaba Causeway ◷ 8.30am-10.30pm ® Churchgate

Konkan Cafe (3, C5)
Mangalorean/Maratha $$$$
Styled like a rustic village kitchen, Konkan Cafe serves dishes from all along the Konkan coast, from Alibaug to Goa and Mangalore. The tasty coastal curries are divided into *sukkhe* (dry) and *olsar* (with gravy).
☎ 56650808 ✉ Taj President Hotel, 90 Cuffe Pde ◷ 12.30-2.45pm & 7-11.45pm ® Churchgate

Leopold Cafe (5, B2)
Café $
Almost every traveller to Colaba makes a visit to the fan-cooled dining room at Leopold for a quick meal or

a chilled bottle of Kingfisher lager. The laid-back ambience is extremely conducive to striking up conversations with strangers and the menu features some memorable Indian and Chinese dishes.
☎ 22020131 ✉ Colaba Causeway ⏰ 8am-midnight ⛾ Churchgate

Ling's Pavilion (5, C1)
Chinese $$$
A massive renovation looks set to raise the reputation of this popular Chinese restaurant even higher. The menu features plenty of familiar mainland and Cantonese food and a hearty and popular Mongolian barbecue. The entrance on Lansdowne Rd (Mahakavi Bhushan Marg) is styled like a Beijing mansion.
☎ 22850023 ✉ 19/12 Lansdowne Rd ⏰ noon-2pm & 6-11pm ⛾ Churchgate

Majestic Hotel (5, B1)
Indian Dhaba $
All that's left of the once majestic Majestic Hotel, this modest thali restaurant regains a bit of dignity by serving the best nonveg thali in Colaba. Order a chai or a salted lime soda to wash it down.
☎ 22835699 ✉ Colaba Causeway ⏰ 7am-11pm ⛾ Churchgate

Ming Palace (5, A4)
Chinese $$
A solid Chinese restaurant with a gregarious doorman and a suitably Chinese interior. Sip wine by the glass and enjoy huge portions of Chinese, Japanese and Korean food under a glittering golden roof.
☎ 22872820 ✉ 73 Apsara Bldg, Colaba Causeway ⏰ 11am-3.30pm & 7-11pm ⛾ Churchgate

Olympia Coffee House (5, B2)
Indian Dhaba $
A window into the past, this mirrored Muslim snack house on Colaba Causeway has all its original 1940s fittings. The cheap lunchtime chicken biryani and *murgh masala* (chicken curry) attracts a hungry, good-natured crowd.
☎ 22021043 ✉ Rahim Mansion, Colaba Causeway ⏰ 7am-midnight ⛾ Churchgate

Tendulkar's (5, C1)
North Indian $$$$
Pet project of Indian cricket star Sachin Tendulkar, this futuristic restaurant is full of ice-white booths and luminescent pillars. The menu features Indian, Chinese and European haute cuisine and Sachin's mum's recipe for Bombay Duck.
☎ 22829934 ✉ 1st fl, Narang House, 34 Chhatrapati Shivaji Marg ⏰ noon-3pm & 7.30-11.45pm ⛾ Churchgate

Thai Pavilion (3, C5)
Thai $$$
For fine Royal Thai food, head to this sophisticated place at the Taj President Hotel. The dining room resembles a Thai royal palace, flavours are delicate and refined and dishes are decorated with carved flower garnishes.
☎ 56650808 ✉ Taj President Hotel, 90 Cuffe Pde ⏰ 12.30-2.45pm & 7-11.45pm ⛾ Churchgate

Laid-back and amiable Leopold Cafe (opposite)

Theobroma (5, A4)
Café $
For muffins, brown bread, sweet cakes and other European breakfast snacks, try this unobtrusive café in the middle of Colaba Causeway. They serve English-style tea and the coffee has quite a zing too.
☎ 56292929 ⊠ Cusrow Baug, Colaba Causeway ⏰ 11am-11pm ⊗ Churchgate

FORT

Fort is busy by day, but empty by night – the busiest areas after hours are Kala Ghoda near K Dubash Marg (Rampart Row) and around Victoria Terminus (Chhatrapati Shivaji Terminus; CST).

Ankur (4, D4)
Indian Seafood $$
Deep in the business district, Ankur serves lip-smacking Mangalorean and Keralan seafood in smart surroundings. Waiters wear bow ties and the fresh prawns, crab and squid add spice to the menu. Expect to wait for a table at lunchtime.
☎ 22654194 ⊠ MP Shetty Marg ⏰ noon-3.30pm & 6-11.30pm ⊗ Churchgate

Apoorva (4, E4)
Indian Seafood $$
Around the corner from the Bombay Store, Apoorva is an upmarket marble seafood restaurant, serving all the ocean's bounty, from curried clams to Bombay Duck. Order a *neer* dosa (coconut and lentil pancake) on the side.
☎ 22870335 ⊠ SA Brelvi Marg ⏰ 11.30am-4pm & 6pm-midnight ⊗ Churchgate

Bharat Lunch Home (4, E3)
Mangalorean $$
Local office workers swear by this Mangalorean restaurant opposite Fort Market. The menu is mainly Mangalorean – we recommend the prawn *gassi* (coconut curry) – but they also serve a refreshingly inexpensive plate of Bombay Duck.
☎ 22618991 ⊠ 317 Bharat House, Shahid Bhagat Singh Marg ⏰ 11.30am-4pm & 5.30pm-midnight ⊗ Churchgate

Britannia & Co (4, F3)
Parsi $
A genuine survivor, Britannia has been serving Parsi favourites to workers in Ballard Estate offices for 80 years. The

interior is modest, with just a handful of wooden tables and chairs, but the food is sensational – try the berry *pulao* (spicy fried rice with chicken and Iranian barberries).
☎ 22615264 ⊠ Shivsagar Ramgulam Marg, Ballard Estate ⏰ 11.30am-4pm Mon-Sat ⊗ CST

Café Coffee Day (4, E2)
Café $
Another big Mumbai coffee chain (see also Barista, p49), Café Coffee Day serves the usual international espresso-based drinks – cappuccinos, lattes, mochas and the like – and sweet cakes. There are branches all over town, including at Chowpatty Beach (3, B3).
☎ 39515909 ⊠ Capital Cinema Bldg, Marzaban Rd ⏰ 8am-midnight ⊗ CST

Chat Masala (4, D5)
Indian Vegetarian $
Traders and brokers celebrate at this upmarket *chat* (Indian-style salad) restaurant opposite the Bombay Stock Exchange. You can sample a huge range of pure-veg Indian salads, from *aloo tikki* (potato with chilli and coriander) to Mumbai's famous *bhelpuri* (Mumbai-style salad).
☎ 56395181 🖳 www .chatmasalaonline.com ⊠ 6/8 Ambalal Doshi Marg ⏰ noon-3.30pm & 6-11.30pm ⊗ Churchgate

Copper Chimney/ Bombay Blue (4, D5)
North & South Indian $$
A Mumbai success story, these conjoined chain restaurants serve popular Indian dishes, fast-food style. The two restaurants offer a

---

PARSI CAFÉS

Hidden away in the backstreets of Fort are a dwindling number of Parsi cafés, established by Zoroastrian refugees who fled to Mumbai from Iran. There used to be dozens of these relaxed eateries, but today just a handful survive, serving traditional Irani cuisine to Mumbai's Parsi community. Some Parsi dishes may already be familiar – dhansak (hot and sour curry with lentils) appears on most British Indian restaurant menus. Good choices include **Britannia & Co** (right), **Jimmy Boy** (opposite) and **Ideal Corner** (opposite).

similar menu and share the same space – turn left for Copper Chimney, the classier of the pair. There's a branch in thePhoenix Mills Shopping Centre (1, A2).
☎ 22021661 ✉ 14 K Dubash Marg ☙ noon-midnight ᯤ Churchgate

Howrah (4, E1)
Bengali $
Where else in Mumbai can you dine under a scale model of Kolkata's Howrah Bridge? Upstairs at New Bengal Hotel, this partly open-air place serves chicken, mutton and seafood in a wide range of Bengali sauces.
☎ 23401976 ✉ Sitaram Bldg, Dr DN Rd ☙ 11.45am-3.45pm & 7pm-midnight ᯤ CST

Ideal Corner (4, D3)
Parsi $
Housed in a former auto workshop near the Residency Hotel, this simple, no-nonsense café serves a different menu of Parsi dishes every day. Come on Wednesday or Friday for the dhansak (hot and sour curry with lentils).
☎ 22621930 ✉ 12 F/G Hornby View, Rustom Sidhwa Marg ☙ 9am-6pm Mon-Sat ᯤ CST

Jimmy Boy (4, E4)
Parsi $
One of just a handful of eateries in the banking district south of Horniman Circle, Jimmy Boy serves tasty Parsi cuisine at reasonable prices. You can splash out on the *lagan nu bhonu*, a traditional Irani wedding feast.
☎ 22700880 ✉ 11 Bank St ☙ 8am-11pm ᯤ Churchgate

BOMBAY DUCK
Bombay Duck is often confused with Peking Duck – to help you out, Bombay Duck is the one that doesn't contain duck. In fact, this unusual dish is prepared from dried fillets of *bombil*, a small bony fish caught in huge numbers along the Konkan coastline. The fillets are re-hydrated and flash fried in a crisp skin of masala spices. The duck part comes from an old nickname for the colonial rulers of Mumbai, corrupted from the Italian word *duces*, meaning ruler.

Joss (4, D5)
Chinese & Southeast Asian $$$
Decorated like a gilded Thai temple, this recent arrival on the Kala Ghoda scene offers an ambitious menu of Chinese, Thai and Southeast Asian dishes, tempered to Indian taste buds – the spicy beef with chillies and garlic goes down a treat.
☎ 56356908 ✉ 30 K Dubash Marg ☙ 12.30-3.30pm & 7.30-11.30pm ᯤ Churchgate

Khyber (4, D5)
Indian $$$$
There can only be one best restaurant in Mumbai, and in our opinion it's Khyber, on Mahatma Gandhi (MG) Rd. Styled like an Afghan palace, this atmospheric eatery is a maze of winding stairs, arched doorways and perforated marble screens. The exciting menu covers a fabulous range of Mughlai and North-West Frontier cuisine. Evening reservations are essential.
☎ 22673227 ✉ 145 MG Rd ☙ 12.30-3.30pm & 7.30-11.30pm ᯤ Churchgate

Mahesh Lunch Home (4, D3)
Indian Seafood $$
A perennial favourite of Mumbai seafood buffs, Mahesh serves top-notch Mangalorean coastal cuisine. The house speciality is *gassi*, a rich seafood curry with coconut and tamarind. There's a branch on Juhu-Tara Rd (2, A1).
☎ 22870938 🖳 www .maheshlunchhome.com ✉ 8B Cawasji Patel St ☙ noon-4pm & 6pm-midnight ᯤ CST

Mocambo Café (4, D3)
European $$
In a split-level dining room with stripy upholstery, Mocambo serves up lunchtime pasta, pizza and grills to busy office workers. Food is reasonably authentic and the bright and airy café ambience fits the city location.

The palatial Khyber

☎ 22870458 ✉ 23A Sir P Mehta Rd 🕑 9am-midnight 🚇 CST

Pratap Lunch Home
(4, D4)
Indian Seafood $
Popular with office workers after hours, Pratap offers a similar seafood menu to the posher 'lunch homes' in the area, but at half the price. Look out for occasional Thai dish on the specials board.
☎ 22871101 ✉ MB House, Janmabhoomi Marg 🕑 11.30am-4pm & 5.30-11.45pm 🚇 Churchgate

Royal China (4, D2)
Chinese $$$$
Full of flickering candles and Chinese *objets d'art*, Royal China offers a stylish dining experience. Shine your shoes, put on your best outfit and come here for the lunchtime dim sum or the duck with plum sauce.
☎ 56355310 ✉ Hajarimal Somani Marg 🕑 noon-3.15pm & 7-11.15pm 🚇 CST

Samovar (4, D5)
Café $
Generations of artists and thinkers have gathered at this café under the Jehangir Art Gallery to discuss art and politics. Sadly its future may be under threat, but for now it continues to serve tasty snacks and cold beers.
☎ 22848000 ✉ Jehangir Art Gallery, 161B MG Rd 🕑 11am-7pm Mon-Sat 🚇 Churchgate

Sher-E-Punjab (4, F2)
Punjabi $$
A handy option near Victoria Terminus or the GPO, Sher-E-Punjab is a smart air-conditioned restaurant serving Punjabi specialities. There's *paneer* (cream cheese) for the vegetarians, and rich chicken and mutton dishes for carnivores. Beers are served at the affiliated permit room (bar) across the road.
☎ 22621188 ✉ 264 Shahid Bhagat Singh Marg 🕑 noon-11.30pm 🚇 CST

Trishna (4, D5)
Indian $$$
One of those old-time places that just keeps getting better with age, Trishna has been Mumbai's favourite seafood restaurant since Sachin Tendulkar was in short trousers. Try the Hyderabadi pomfret and *koliwala* (fisherman's style) prawns.
☎ 22614991 ✉ 4 Sai Baba Marg 🕑 noon-3.30pm & 6.30pm-midnight 🚇 Churchgate

Vithal Bhelwala (4, E2)
Indian-Style Salads $
If you don't want to risk the *bhelpuri* stands at Chowpatty Beach, you can enjoy it in air-conditioned comfort in this smart 1950s-style snack bar near the Sterling Cinema. The menu's other options include ice cream and samosas.
☎ 56317211 ✉ 5 AK Naik Marg 🕑 11am-11pm 🚇 CST

CHURCHGATE

Veer Nariman Rd is the centre of the action in Churchgate but be warned – most places are mobbed every night and you may need to wait for a table.

Gaylord (4, B4)
North Indian/Continental $$$
Open since the early 1950s, Gaylord is a Mumbai institution. The wrought iron, potted palms and waiters in cummerbunds add a touch of the Raj and the Indian and continental food is consistently reliable. It's not a bad spot for an evening drink either.
☎ 22821259 ✉ Mayfair Bldg, Veer Nariman Rd 🕑 noon-3pm & 7-11.30pm 🚇 Churchgate

Indian Summer (4, B4)
North Indian $$
With smartly dressed waiters and a resident *paan*-wallah by the door, Indian Summer is a relaxing place to enjoy veg and nonveg cuisine. The filling lunchtime buffet costs Rs 270 and is worth every paise.
☎ 22835445 💻 www.indiansummerindia.com ✉ 80 Veer Nariman Rd 🕑 noon-3.30pm & 7pm-midnight 🚇 Churchgate

Mocha (4, B4)
Café $
Barista may be slicker, but Mocha is where young Mumbaikers come for their caffeine hit. There's a chilled-out Moroccan kasbah vibe, and you can sip on cappuccinos and beers or puff yourself silly on a hookah pipe for Rs 150. There's a branch on Juhu-Tara Rd (2, A1).
☎ 56336070 ✉ Veer Nariman Rd 🕑 9am-1.30pm 🚇 Churchgate

Pearl of the Orient
(4, B4)
Chinese $$$$
See the bright lights of Marine Dr (Netaji Subhashchandra Bose Marg) spin around

High tea: orange pekoe tea and scones at the Tea Centre

you from this revolving restaurant atop the Ambassador Hotel. The Chinese food is superior, but the bill can soon mount up once you add the luxury taxes.
☎ 22041131 ✉ Ambassador Hotel, Veer Nariman Rd ☾ 1.30-3.30pm & 7.30-11.30pm ⊛ Churchgate

Pizza Express (4, B4)
Pizza $$$
The Mumbai branch of Pizza Express serves up all your pizza favourites, from *margherita* to *quattro stagioni* (four seasons), in a smart dining room on Churchgate's main drag. The pizzas here are better than those at Pizzeria down the road.
☎ 56828106 ✉ 80 Veer Nariman Rd ☾ noon-midnight ⊛ Churchgate

Pizzeria (4, A4)
Pizza $$
Overlooking the sea on the corner of Marine Dr and Veer Nariman Rd, this popular pizza parlour serves pizzas at a furious rate to a chattering, middle-class crowd. Take your pick from more traditional toppings such as pepperoni and pineapple or go Indian with tandoori chicken.

☎ 22856115 ✉ 143 Marine Dr ☾ noon-12.30am ⊛ Churchgate

Samrat (4, B5)
Gujarati $$
A smart veg restaurant with bas-relief on the walls, aircon and Gujarati thalis on the menu. The calm interior is a breath of fresh air after the bustling streets outside.
☎ 22820022 ✉ Prem Court, J Tata Rd ☾ noon-10.30pm ⊛ Churchgate

Tea Centre (4, B4)
Café $
Run by the India Tea Board, this quaint tea shop is the perfect place for an afternoon high tea. Waiters in turbans serve up scones and tea in silver teapots.

Topping the bill is the Fine Tippy Golden Flowery Orange Pekoe (Rs 90 per pot) from Darjeeling.
☎ 22819142 ✉ Resham Bhawan, 78 Veer Nariman Rd ☾ 8am-11pm ⊛ Churchgate

CHOWPATTY & KALBADEVI

As well as Chowpatty's famous *bhelpuri* stands, there are several excellent cafés and restaurants close to the beach.

By the Way (3, B2)
Café $
Run by the Seva Sadan, a charitable organisation that cares for disadvantaged women, this canteen-style café serves veg and nonveg fast food including a handful of Western and Parsi dishes, and big slices of apple pie.
☎ 23803532 ✉ Pandita Ramabhai Rd ☾ 11am-11pm ⊛ Grant Road

Cafe Ideal (3, B3)
North Indian $
A quiet beachfront snack house, serving North Indian staples and cold beers

BHELPURI
Chowpatty Beach is the best place in Mumbai to sample the traditional Mumbai salad, *bhelpuri*, a tangy mixture of crisp chickpea-flour noodles, puffed rice, green mango, coriander, onion, potato, peanuts, chilli and sweet tamarind chutney. The *bhelpuri* trade used to be dominated by wandering vendors, but these days you can buy it fresh from permanent booths on Chowpatty Beach. Other popular Chowpatty snacks to look out for include *panipuri* (puffed *puris* – fried bread – filled with dhal) and *ragda puri* (*puri* with spiced peas).

GREAT VIEWS

For panoramic views over Churchgate and Marine Dr, head to **Pearl of the Orient** (p54). More modest sea views are afforded by **Kandahar** (p59), **Revival** (right) and **Pizzeria** (p55).

straight from the fridge. The food isn't bad and sea breezes blow in through the windows.
☎ 23630943 ✉ Chowpatty Seaface ⏱ 10am-10pm 🚇 Charni Road

Cream Centre (3, B3)
International $$$
There's *always* a queue at this astoundingly popular restaurant so allow an extra half-hour while you wait for a table. Inside you can feast on everything from nachos to Russian salad. There's a branch on Linking Rd (2, C2).
☎ 23679222 🖳 www .creamcentre.com ✉ 25B Chowpatty Seaface ⏱ noon-midnight 🚇 Charni Road

New Kulfi Centre (3, B3)
Ice Cream $
For freshly churned kulfi (Indian ice cream flavoured with cardamom) in a variety of tasty configurations, try this hole-in-the-wall ice creamery facing Chowpatty Beach. There's normally a queue and they do a mean *falooda* (rose-flavoured milk with vermicelli noodles).
✉ Chowpatty Seaface ⏱ 10am-10pm 🚇 Charni Road

Rajdhani (3, D3)
North Indian $
It's worth breaking away from the seafront to hunt down this small but perfectly-formed thali

restaurant in the alleys north of Crawford Market. The Gujarati, Maharashtran and Rajasthani thalis are reputed to be the best in town.
☎ 23449014 ✉ Sheikh Memon St ⏱ noon-4pm & 7-10.30pm 🚇 Masjid

Revival (3, B3)
Indian Vegetarian $$
With a swish, theatrical-themed dining room looking out over Chowpatty Beach, this upmarket vegetarian restaurant is a fine alternative to the ever-popular Cream Centre. The food is good and there's a generous lunch buffet on Sunday for Rs 325.
☎ 23637834 ✉ Chowpatty Seaface ⏱ noon-3.30pm & 7-11.30pm 🚇 Charni Road

BANDRA

Waterfield Rd in Bandra is fast becoming Mumbai's premier dining strip. However, the Bandra diners are notoriously faddish and restaurants open and vanish almost overnight. The following places are well established, but ask locally to see if any must-visit restaurants have opened up.

China Gate (2, C2)
Chinese $$
A tiled pagoda roof marks the entrance to this swish Chinese restaurant. Surprise yourself with the 'woolly

chicken' (tender chicken breast fried with garlic and chillies). This place is justifiably popular and reservations are essential at weekends.
☎ 26432570 ✉ 155 Waterfield Rd ⏱ noon-4pm & 7pm-12.30am 🚇 Bandra

Dosa Diner (2, C2)
South Indian $
A less-expensive choice in glitzy Bandra, Dosa Diner offers a tasty range of dosas (lentil-flour pancakes) and veg curries, with a special menu for kids. We recommend the *neer* dosa topped with spicy potato masala.
☎ 26404488 ✉ cnr Turner & Waterfield Rds ⏱ 11.30am-11.30pm 🚇 Bandra

Just Around the Corner (2, B2)
International $
This is fast food, Indian-style; Just Around the Corner serves up a range of pizzas, burgers, pasta and salads as well as various Indian and Chinese toppings scooped into foot-long subs. It operates like a school canteen –

Kids' favourite: Dosa Diner

just grab a tray and choose whatever you want from the counter.
☎ 26006717 ✉ cnr 24th & 30th Rds ☟ 8am-12.45am 🚇 Bandra

Moti Mahal (2, C2)
North Indian $$
Starched white tablecloths, suited waiters, and a vast menu of Mughlai delights help raise this place above the competition. Break out of the mould and try some of the more unusual kebabs from the tandoor on offer here.
☎ 26408577 ✉ cnr Turner & Waterfield Rds ☟ noon-4pm & 7-11pm 🚇 Bandra

Olive Bar & Kitchen (2, A2)
Mediterranean $$$$
Worth the excursion to Pali Hill, Olive is one of the trendiest eateries in town. It serves wholesome Mediterranean dishes drizzled with olive oil to Mumbai yuppies and Bollywood stars. Dress to impress if you want to fit in.
☎ 26058228 ✉ Pali Hill Tourist Hotel, 14 Union Park ☟ 12.30-6pm & 7.30pm-2am 🚇 Bandra

Thai Ban (2, A3)
Thai $$
On a narrow food street west of Waterfield Rd, Thai Ban is a tasy neighbourhood Thai. The interior is plain but the excellent menu of Thai curries, salads and stir-fries more than makes up for it.
☎ 26458176 ✉ Gaspar Enclave, Dr Ambedkar Rd ☟ noon-4.30pm & 7-11.45pm 🚇 Bandra

Zenzi (2, C2)
French/Asian $$$
By day, a restaurant; by night, a trendy lounge bar. Beautiful young things flock to Zenzi for the gourmet French and Indochinese food, and for the street cred. It's a good place to road test that new Krishna Mehta shirt.

TRY THE HOUSE RED?
Wine is fast becoming the beverage of choice for Mumbai yuppies. The rapidly expanding Indian wine industry is centred on the Maharashtran town of Nashik, which has gently sloping hills that are perfect for French grape varieties such as Cabernet Sauvignon, Shiraz, Chenin Blanc and Chardonnay. Major vineyards include Sula, Grover and Chateau Indage; the latter also produces a home-grown Indian champagne. If you fancy a few bottles to take home, try **Shah Wines** (4, E1; ☎ 23427996; Dr DN Rd), near Crawford Market.

MAGIC MANGO

Once a year in early May, Mumbai goes crazy for Alphonso mangoes, arguably the sweetest and tastiest mango in the world. During harvest season these small but perfectly formed mangoes are sold in incredible numbers from shops, markets, street vendors and overloaded fruit carts all over Mumbai. The city even holds an Alphonso mango festival in Juhu at the start of May – celebrated by the consumption of huge numbers of mangoes. Interestingly, the Alphonso takes its name from Affonso d'Albuquerque, the former Portuguese governor of the Konkan Coast.

☎ 56430670 🖳 www
.zenzi-india.com ✉ 183
Waterfield Rd 🕑 noon-
1.30am 🚇 Bandra

JUHU

As well as the following restaurants, there are numerous food stalls and *bhelpuri* stands on Juhu Beach, near the Ramada Palm Grove Hotel.

Don Giovanni (2, A1)
Italian $$
Run by an Italian immigrant family, this old-fashioned bistro has Chianti bottles on the walls and a hearty menu of home-style Italian cooking. Go for homemade pasta or treat yourself to some hearty village stews and bakes.
☎ 26153125 🖳 www
.dongiovanniristorante.com
✉ Hotel Bawa Continental,
Juhu-Tara Rd 🕑 12.30-
2.40pm & 7.30-11.40pm
🚇 Vile Parle

Govinda's Restaurant
(2, A1)
Indian Vegetarian $$
Visitors and guests at Juhu's Hare Krishna temple can enjoy

a lunch and dinner buffet of veg dishes, accompanied by fresh fruit juices, buttermilk and *jal jeera* (lemon water flavoured with cumin).
☎ 26200337 ✉ Hare
Krishna Land, Juhu Church Rd
🕑 12.30-3.30pm & 7.30-
10.30pm 🚇 Vile Parle

Little Italy (2, A2)
Italian $$$
The Italian chef at this smart bistro cooks up an impressive assortment of vegetarian pasta, pizzas and *secondi piatti* (second courses) using fresh local produce and imported Italian mozzarella and parmesan. Light eaters can choose to plump for bruschetta and *crostini* (grilled bread with herbs,

cheese and various other toppings).
☎ 56923266 ✉ www
.littleitaly-india.com ✉ 18B
Juhu-Tara Rd 🕑 noon-3pm
& 7-11.30pm 🚇 Vile Parle

Lotus Café (2, A1)
Multicuisine $$$
Set in the huge, airy foyer of the Marriott hotel, Lotus Café offers one of the best buffets in Mumbai. You can come for breakfast, lunch or dinner and enjoy a mixture of slow-cooked curries and dishes cooked on the spot.
☎ 56933277 ✉ JW
Marriott, Juhu-Tara Rd
🕑 6.30am-12.30am
🚇 Vile Parle

WORTH A TRIP

There are several fantastic restaurants located away from the main tourist hangouts; getting to the following restaurants will involve a taxi and/or train ride.

Culture Curry (1, A2)
South Indian $$
Goa Portuguesa's partner restaurant, Culture Curry serves food from across South India, from Hyderabad to the tip of Kerala. Seafood fans can sample lobster in a

JUST DESSERTS

Wherever people gather in Mumbai, you'll find vendors selling sweet treats such as kulfi (Indian ice cream flavoured with cardamom), *gulab jamin* (dough balls soaked in rose syrup), *falooda* (rose-flavoured milk with vermicelli noodles) and *gola* (crushed ice with fruit syrup). Sadly, the desserts available on the streets are often too bacterially active for Western stomachs, but you can find these delights at most Mumbai restaurants.

mustard curry sauce, while vegetarians have the option of banana cooked with pepper and tamarind.
☎ 24440202 ✉ Kataria Rd, Lower Parel 🕒 noon-3.30pm & 7pm-12.30am 🚇 Matunga Road

Dakshin (2, B1)
South Indian $$$$
Bedecked with flowers, temple bells and wooden carvings, Dakshin showcases the delicious cuisines of Kerala, Tamil Nadu, Andhra Pradesh and Karnataka. The atmosphere is casual and the food is sublime – don't miss the unusual Carnatic desserts.
☎ 28303030 ✉ ITC Grand Maratha Sheraton, Sahar Airport Rd, Sahar 🕒 12.30-2.45pm & 7.30-11.45pm 🚇 Vile Parle

Frangipani (3, C4)
Italian $$$$
The Hilton Towers' Italian restaurant is bright and open plan, with a sophisticated menu of pasta, grilled meats and wood-fired pizzas. The complimentary fresh-baked bread for dunking in vinegar and olive oil is a nice touch.
☎ 56324343 ✉ Hilton Towers, Marine Dr, Nariman Point 🕒 noon-11.45pm 🚇 Churchgate

Goa Portuguesa (1, A2)
Goan $$
Several places in Mumbai try their hand at Goan food, but Goa Portuguesa really excels. Expect stained glass, waiters in Hawaiian shirts and seafood in spicy, coconutty sauces. To get here take the train to Matunga Road

station and head towards the hospital.
☎ 24440202 ✉ Kataria Rd, Lower Parel 🕒 noon-3.30pm & 7pm-12.30am 🚇 Matunga Road

India Jones (3, C4)
Asian $$$$
The walls are decorated with Chinese calligraphy at this *über*-sophisticated hotel restaurant. The menu hopscotches around Asia, from Cambodia and Thailand to Japan, China and Korea, and every nuance and detail has been artfully conceived and executed.
☎ 56326330 ✉ Hilton Towers, Marine Dr, Nariman Point 🕒 12.30-2.45pm & 7.30-11.45pm 🚇 Churchgate

Jewel of India (3, B1)
North Indian $$$$
Tucked under the Nehru Centre, this sophisticated restaurant serves top-class Mughlai nosh to well-heeled Breach Candy families. The Rs 450 lunchtime buffet features dozens of vegetarian and nonvegetarian dishes and it attracts a massive crowd.
☎ 24949435 ✉ Nehru Centre, Dr Annie Besant Rd, Worli 🕒 12.30-3pm & 7.30pm-midnight 🚇 Mahalaxmi

Kandahar (3, C4)
North Indian $$$$
Sea views, Afghan rugs and a menu of Mughlai delights make Kandahar one

of Mumbai's great dining experiences. Topping the menu are the tandoori *jhinga* (monster prawns), but almost everything from the tandoor is mouthwateringly delicious.
☎ 56326210 ✉ Oberoi Hotel, Nariman Point 🕒 12.30-3pm & 7.30-11.30pm 🚇 Churchgate

Pan-Asian (2, B1)
Asian $$$$
One of three glorious restaurants at the ITC Grand Maratha Sheraton, Pan-Asian cooks up dishes from across Asia, from Burmese salads to Japanese *yakitori* (barbecue skewers). It's a stylish place with an entrance that resembles a bamboo forest.
☎ 28303030 ✉ ITC Grand Maratha Sheraton, Sahar Airport Rd, Sahar 🕒 7-11.45pm 🚇 Vile Parle

Peshawri (2, B1)
North Indian $$$$
The ITC's atmospheric Mughlai restaurant puts a tandoor to good use, preparing rich and satisfying dishes originating from the North-West Frontier. Meat dominates the menu here but vegetarians can find *paneer* and fresh vegetables cooked with the same panache.
☎ 28303030 ✉ ITC Grand Maratha Sheraton, Sahar Airport Rd, Sahar 🕒 12.30-2.45pm & 7.30-11.45pm 🚇 Vile Parle

BUSINESS DINING
To impress clients, book a table at **Khyber** (p53), **Peshawri** (right), or **Golden Dragon** (p50).

Entertainment

Nightlife in Mumbai is fast and frenetic. New places open in a trice and go under just as quickly. Lounge bars are the latest big thing in Mumbai and more and more bars are stripping out the tables and chairs and replacing them with comfy divans. Then there are the hotel nightclubs – huge, showy affairs where attitude and appearance are everything. For a quieter drink, there are plenty of restaurant-bars and student-oriented cafés where you can quench your thirst and actually have a conversation.

Officially, alcohol can only be served to over 21s, but foreigners are rarely asked for ID. City regulations prohibit the sale of alcohol after 1.30am, but many bars and clubs in the suburbs push on till 3am at weekends. Many restaurants double as drinking holes – handy if you want a drink without paying a cover charge. If you do want to party till dawn with the beautiful people, set aside at least Rs 1000 for entry fees to nightclubs and lounge bars.

Nightspots are dotted across Mumbai. The Colaba area has noisy cafés, nightclubs and sophisticated lounge bars that attract a mixed local and foreign crowd. Veer Nariman Rd is where the action is in Churchgate and there are several drinking holes hidden away in Fort. Recenly the attention has shifted north to Bandra and Juhu, which are full of cutting-edge bars and restaurants. Another up-and-coming party place is the Phoenix Mills Shopping Centre on Senapati Bhapat Marg in Lower Parel.

STAGS & LADY STAGS

To discourage moral turpitude, Mumbai's nightclubs have strict rules for singles on the prowl. Most clubs only admit couples, which can leave lone revellers at something of a loose end. Stags – as single men are known locally – are only accepted at a handful of clubs and both male and female stags pay the same high entry fees as couples. To get around this proscription, do as the locals do and tag along with a friend of the opposite gender.

For the latest listings and entertainment news, pick up *Mid-Day,* the *Times of India* or the Mumbai edition of *Time Out* magazine. Another comprehensive source of things to do in Mumbai after hours is the *Times Nightlife & Leisure Guide* sold with the *Times Food Guide* in local bookshops for Rs 150.

Cartoons and chilled beer at Cafe Mondegar (opposite)

BARS & PUBS

Bayview Bar (3, C4)
At the Oberoi on Marine Dr (Netaji Subhashchandra Bose Marg), this is a traditional bar, with a long list of spirits and old-fashioned cocktails (try the Cosmopolitan) and sea views. Order a cigar and relive the Raj.
☎ 56326220 ✉ Oberoi Hotel, Marine Dr, Nariman Point ⑤ free ⏰ 5pm-1am 🚇 Churchgate

Bed Lounge & Bar (2, C2)
Leading the lounge bar revolution, the Bed Lounge is full of sumptuously uphol-stered divans, gilded mirrors and Ottoman trim. Cocktails dominate the drinks menu and there's a chill-out area on the roof if the noise and bustle gets too much.
☎ 39535544 ✉ Linking Rd, Bandra ⑤ couple/male/female Rs 1000/1000/500, Sat all Rs 1500 ⏰ 8pm-1.30am 🚇 Bandra

Bombay High (2, B1)
Reminiscent of the hotel bar in *Lost in Translation,* Bombay High is a cheesy but cheer-ful, business-oriented place at the ITC Grand Maratha Sheraton. A suitably mellow live duo performs covers from 9pm on Friday.
☎ 28303030 ✉ ITC Grand Maratha Sheraton, Sahar Airport Rd, Sahar ⑤ free ⏰ 11am-12.30am 🚇 Vile Parle

Busaba (5, B2)
Next door to Indigo (p62), Busaba is a moody, dimly lit lounge bar with an '80s Vegas vibe. Downstairs you'll find comfy chairs and

cocktails, while upstairs is a partly open-air dining area. The resident DJ rocks till late on Friday night.
☎ 22043779 🖥 www.busa bong.com ✉ 4 Mandlik Rd, Colaba ⑤ after midnight Rs 200 ⏰ 7am-1am, till 4am Fri 🚇 Churchgate

Cafe Mondegar (5, B1)
Another packed Colaba drinking spot, this café on the corner of Colaba Causeway (Shahid Bhagat Singh Marg) and Lansdowne Rd (Ma-hakavi Bhushan Marg) serves hundreds of bottles of chilled beer to locals and foreigners every evening. There's a tiny air-conditioned room at the back for a more chilled-out (ahem) drinking experience.
☎ 22020591 ✉ 5A Colaba Causeway, Colaba ⑤ free ⏰ 8am-12.30am 🚇 Churchgate

Dome (4, A3)
At the Intercontinental Hotel, Dome is a calm but classy open-air bar with a slow, easy mood and epic views along Marine Dr. Bring someone you love and mut-ter sweet nothings under the moonlight.
☎ 39879999 ✉ Intercon-tinental Hotel, 135 Marine Dr, Churchgate ⑤ free ⏰ 6.30am-12.30am 🚇 Churchgate

Gallops (3, C1)
Winners and losers gather at this posh bar and restaurant at the Mahalaxmi Race Course to celebrate big wins and drown their sorrows after big losses. Mobile phones must be left with security at the racecourse gates to prevent cheating.

☎ 23071448 ✉ Mahal-axmi Race Course, Keshavrao Khadye Marg, Mahalaxmi ⑤ free ⏰ 11am-midnight 🚇 Mahalaxmi

Gaylord (4, B4)
This popular Raj-style restaurant in the middle of Veer Nariman Rd is a recommended choice for a grown-up drink. Order a gin and tonic, sit back in a wicker chair and contemplate how far India has come since 1947.
☎ 22821259 ✉ Mayfair Bldg, Veer Nariman Rd, Churchgate ⑤ free ⏰ noon-3pm & 7-11.30pm 🚇 Churchgate

Geoffrey's (4, A4)
Somewhere between an English pub and the bar in *Cheers,* Geoffrey's is one of the more relaxing hotel bars in town. The atmosphere is jovial and corporate and it pulls in a good-natured, mixed crowd.
☎ 22851212 ✉ Hotel Marine Plaza, 29 Marine Dr, Churchgate ⑤ free ⏰ 11.30am-1.30am 🚇 Churchgate

Ghetto (3, B1)
A dark, grungy cavern of a place, with graffiti on the walls and Bollywood hits on the sound system. It's couples only but female stags may be able to talk their way past the doorman.
☎ 23538418 ✉ 30B Bhu-labhai Desai Marg, Breach Candy ⑤ free ⏰ 7.30pm-1.30am 🚇 Grant Hill

Gokul Restaurant & Permit Room (5, B1)
It may be dark, scruffy and male dominated, but Gokul charges half as much for

SHEESHA FEATURES
More and more Mumbai bars are adding *sheesha* pipes to the list of intoxicants available to patrons. The strong, fruit-flavoured tobacco creates a feeling of light-headedness and general wellbeing, which can't always be said for the strong spirits favoured by traditional drinkers. Top spots for a puff include **Mocha** (right), **Karma** (right) and **Olive Bar & Kitchen** (right).

beers and spirits as other bars in Colaba. Take a seat at one of the Formica tables and order something from a long list of Indian beers and shots.
☎ 22848248 ✉ 10 Tulloch Rd, Colaba $ free ⏰ 11.30am-12.30am 🚇 Churchgate

Indigo (5, B2)
South Mumbai's best European restaurant is also a great spot to sip a long drink and observe Mumbai high society going about its business. As well as beers and flowery cocktails, you can sample a fantastic range of local and imported wines by the bottle or glass.
☎ 56368980 ✉ 4 Mandlik Rd, Colaba $ free ⏰ noon-3pm & 7.30pm-midnight 🚇 Churchgate

Indus Cocktail Bar (5, B2)
After hours, the restaurant at the Hotel Diplomat becomes a buzzing cocktail bar where bright young things come to rub shoulders with out-of-towners. Order the 'Flaming Lamborghini' just to find out what it is!
☎ 22021661 ✉ Hotel Diplomat, 24-26 Mereweather Rd, Colaba $ free ⏰ noon-1am 🚇 Churchgate

Karma (3, B3)
On SV Patel Marg (Sandhurst Rd), Karma is one of few places to drink near Chowpatty Beach. It's part bar, part restaurant, with a chill-out area full of hookahs and comfy divans. It also serves decent Indian grub.
☎ 23617171 ✉ 534 SV Patel Marg, Chowpatty $ free ⏰ noon-1.30am 🚇 Charni Road

Leopold Cafe (5, B2)
The most popular drinking hole in Colaba, Leopold serves giant bottles of Indian beer and local wines in a nostalgic fan-cooled dining room. The air-conditioned room upstairs is mainly reserved for Indian couples. Wherever you sit, you'll have to pay for drinks at the time you order.
☎ 22020131 ✉ Colaba Causeway, Colaba $ free ⏰ 8am-midnight 🚇 Churchgate

Mocha (4, B4)
Churchgate's trendiest coffee shop doubles as Churchgate's trendiest bar. Order a glass of Indian plonk and a hookah, sit back in an easy chair and watch Mumbai go by. There's a branch on Juhu-Tara Rd (2, A1).
☎ 56336070 ✉ Veer Nariman Rd, Churchgate

$ free ⏰ 9am-1.30am 🚇 Churchgate

Olive Bar & Kitchen (2, A2)
Trend-setting and fantastically popular with Mumbai's social elite and social climbers, Olive is a Mediterranean restaurant by day and a bustling terrace bar by night. It's *the* place in town to rub noses with the bright lights of Bollywood, but scruffy drinkers won't make it past the style gurus on the door.
☎ 26058228 ✉ Pali Hill Tourist Hotel, 14 Union Park, Bandra $ free ⏰ 12.30-6pm & 7.30pm-2am 🚇 Bandra

Opium Den (3, C4)
Full of chinoiserie, tinkling water features and soft, divan seating, Opium Den is better than your average hotel bar. The quiet booths are great places to conduct business and it's a wonderfully calm place to sit with a book.
☎ 56325757 ✉ Hilton Towers, Marine Dr, Nariman Point $ free ⏰ 12.30pm-1.30am 🚇 Churchgate

Hookah at Mocha

Provogue Lounge (1, A2)
Provogue Lounge is extremely fashion conscious, as you might expect from a bar set in a designer-clothes store. After hours, the clothes are packed away and glam bar staff serve up exotic mocktails and cocktails.
☎ 24972525 ✉ High Street Phoenix, 462 Senapati Bhapat Marg, Lower Parel 💲 before/after 11pm Rs 500/1000 🕑 10.30pm-1.30am Mon-Sat 🚇 Lower Parel

Rain Bar & Eatery (2, A1)
Juhu's biggest contribution to the party scene, this partly al fresco restaurant-bar is decorated with dark wood, glow lamps and water features. However, the place does take some hunting down — you'll find the entrance opposite the Ramee Guestline Hotel.
☎ 26239217 ✉ 14 Silver Beach Estate, AB Nair Rd, Juhu 💲 free 🕑 8pm-1.30am 🚇 Vile Parle

Red Light (4, D5)
A single red traffic light is the only external sign of this dark and moody lounge bar on the corner of K Dubash Marg (Rampart Row) and Mahatma Gandhi (MG) Rd. Inside everything is red and black and the dance floor throbs to dance, trance and hip-hop. There are regular guest DJs from local record labels.
☎ 56346249 ✉ cnr K Dubash Marg & MG Rd, Fort 💲 couple/male/female Wed & Sat Rs 800/800/400, Sun Rs 600/600/300 🕑 7pm-1.30am 🚇 Churchgate

Seijo & the Soul Dish (2, C2)
When it comes to style, nowhere comes close to Seijo. It has a futuristic Japanese-style bar with Manga cartoons on the walls and an outdoor terrace with toilets in space-age wooden pods. The entrance is next to the ICICI bank.
☎ 26405555 ✉ 2nd flr, 206 Krystal, Waterfield Rd, Bandra 💲 couple/stag Fri Rs 200, Sat Rs 500 🕑 7pm-1.30am 🚇 Bandra

Toto's Garage (2, B2)
Not every bar in Bandra is ultratrendy. Set in a former auto-repair shop, Toto's has wrenches and dismantled engines decorating the walls and a VW car above the bar. The crowd is older and officey.

LIVE IN MUMBAI
Live music is fairly thin on the ground in Mumbai, but local bands strut their stuff at **Not Just Jazz by the Bay** (4, A4; ☎ 22851876; Veer Nariman Rd; Wed-Thu Rs 150, Fri-Sun Rs 200; 🕑 6pm-2am) in Churchgate. From Wednesday to Saturday, live bands play everything from Bollywood pop to Western rock, and you can sing along to your favourite *masti* (fun) hits on the karaoke machine from Sunday to Tuesday.

HOTEL BARS

All of Mumbai's upmarket hotels have their own bars, but most are dreary places with empty chairs and insipid piped Muzak. However, there are exceptions. **Opium Den** (p62) at the Hilton Towers, **Bayview Bar** (p61) at the Oberoi Hotel and **Geoffrey's** (p61) at Hotel Marine Plaza are genuinely welcoming places for a business drink. Alternatively, why not wallow in the cheesy hotel-bar mood? **Bombay High** (p61) at the ITC Grand Maratha Sheraton has Scottish single malt whiskeys on the menu and a duo playing soporific jazz covers every Friday.

☎ 26005494 ✉ 30th Rd, Bandra 💲 free 🕐 6pm-12.30am 🚇 Bandra

View Bar (1, A2)
Part of the bowling alley in the Phoenix Mills Shopping Centre, this brightly lit American-style sports bar serves a large selection of imported wines, beers and spirits. View Bar pulls in a friendly office crowd, but don't expect it to do any favours for your bowling aim.
☎ 24914000 ✉ Phoenix Mills Shopping Centre, 462 Senapati Bhapat Marg, Lower Parel 💲 free 🕐 noon-1.30am 🚇 Lower Parel

Voodoo Pub (5, B4)
Saturday at Voodoo is the only gay night in Mumbai and it draws a friendly, low-key local crowd (a necessity as homosexuality is still technically illegal in India). Other nights the bar is mostly empty.
☎ 22841959 ✉ Kamal Mansion, Arthur Bunder Rd, Colaba 💲 Rs 250 🕐 8.30pm-1.30am 🚇 Churchgate

Zenzi (2, C2)
Futuristic orange and grey décor and a 'sit back and chill' attitude have made Zenzi one of Bandra's favourite bars. There's a terrace with easy chairs and bamboo plants, or you can drink inside in the lounge bar and restaurant.
☎ 56430670 ✉ 183 Waterfield Rd, Bandra 💲 free 🕐 noon-1.30am 🚇 Bandra

NIGHTCLUBS

Almost all of Mumbai's nightclubs are inside luxury hotels so smart dress is a prerequisite for a big night out. Couples are generally preferred, but most clubs will admit stags and lady stags who seem reasonably well behaved.

Enigma (2, A1)
Dominated by a sparkling crystal chandelier, the JW Marriott's nightclub shakes to the sound of house and Hindi pop until the early hours. You can sample Enigma's bewildering array of wines, cocktails and cigars and afterwards stroll out to watch the dawn on Juhu Beach.
☎ 56933000 ✉ JW Marriott, Juhu-Tara Rd, Juhu 💲 Mon-Fri Rs 1000, Sat & Sun Rs 1500 🕐 9pm-3am Wed-Sun 🚇 Vile Parle

Insomnia (5, C2)
Insomnia is deeply cool and it knows it. This glitzy nightclub at the Taj Mahal Palace & Tower attracts the cream of the cream and well-behaved stags are welcome. Taj guests are spared the hefty cover charge.
☎ 56653366 ✉ Taj Mahal Palace & Tower, Apollo Bunder, Colaba 💲 per couple/stag Rs 600, Sat & Sun Rs 1000 🕐 9.30pm-1.30am Tue-Sun 🚇 Churchgate

POOL BARS

The best choice for pool and snooker fans is **Sport 'n' Spirits** (4, D2; ☎ 22077270; Marzaban Rd, Fort; 🕐 11am-midnight). Budding Stephen Hendrys can choose between the air-conditioned 1st-floor lounge and the partly open-air rooftop pool hall; tables cost Rs 50 per frame. Another decent choice is the **Sports Bar** (5, C1; ☎ 56396681; Colaba Causeway, Colaba; 🕐 8am-1.30am), in the Regal Cinema building, which has one full-sized table and international sports on the big-screen TV. There's also a branch in the Phoenix Mills Shopping Centre (1, A2).

Lush Lounge & Grille
(1, A2)
This New York–style lounge bar is full of brushed steel surfaces and air-kissing, phone-texting socialites. Stock up on designer fashions at the Quorum centre next door before you come.
☎ 56634601 ✉ Phoenix Mills Shopping Centre, 462 Senapati Bhapat Marg, Lower Parel 💲 Sun-Thu Rs 800, Fri & Sat Rs 1000 🕑 7pm-1.30am 🚇 Lower Parel

Polly Esther's (5, C1)
Cocktail umbrellas, lava lamps, waiters in Afro wigs – Polly Esther's proudly embraces the 1970s and Mumbai loves her for it. Leave your khakis and your inhibitions at the door and enjoy the retro indulgence. Stags are admitted on Thursday.
☎ 22871122 ✉ Gordon House Hotel, 5 Battery St, Colaba 💲 per couple/stag Rs 600, per couple Fri/Sat

Positive vibes, Polly Esther's

Rs 800/900 🕑 9pm-1.30am Tue-Sat 🚇 Churchgate

Ra (1, A2)
If you don't have an hour-glass figure or perfect pecs, you may feel slightly intimidated at this glass-roofed lounge bar in High Street Phoenix. It's a restaurant by day, but it bursts into life after 7pm, when the beautiful people come out to party under the stars.
☎ 56614343 ✉ High Street Phoenix, 462 Senapati Bhapat Marg, Lower Parel 💲 Fri & Sat Rs 1200 🕑 7pm-1.30am 🚇 Lower Parel

Velocity (3, B2)
The most happening place in Breach Candy, Velocity is upstairs in an anonymous office building on Tardeo Rd, almost opposite the school for the blind. The décor is techno-industrial and three rooms play booming dance, trance, hip-hop and '70s music.
☎ 23514343 ✉ 2nd flr, Film Centre, Tardeo Rd, Haji Ali 💲 per couple/stag Rs 800/600, Wed Rs 600/400 🕑 9.30pm-1.30am Wed, Fri & Sat 🚇 Mumbai Central

Zaha (2, B1)
Light-up tables and long sofas add to the lounge vibe at this posh nightspot at the Leela Kempinski hotel. The Chateau Indage wine label is one of the backers of this club so expect plenty of Indian wines on the menu.
☎ 56911338 ✉ Leela Kempinski, Sahar Airport Rd, Sahar 💲 Mon-Fri Rs 700, Sat & Sun Rs 1000 🕑 9pm-3am 🚇 Vile Parle

CINEMAS

Mumbai has dozens of cinemas screening the latest Bollywood blockbusters. The following cinema halls also show imported Hollywood blockbusters.

Eros Cinema (4, C4)
A gorgeous Art Deco cinema with a glorious rocket-shaped façade. Punters come here for Bollywood smashes and a smaller number of Hollywood imports. After the flick, stroll along Veer Nariman Rd for a meal or a beer.
☎ 22822335 ✉ cnr J Tata Rd & Maharshi Karve Rd, Churchgate 💲 Rs 40-80 🚇 Churchgate

MUMBAI INTERNATIONAL FILM FESTIVAL

On one level, there's a film festival every week in Mumbai – Bollywood studios churn out dozens of new movies every week – but it's well worth checking out the documentaries, shorts and animation at the annual Mumbai International Film Festival every January, organised by the Indian Ministry of Broadcasting & Information – see www.filmsdivision.org for details.

Inox Cinema (4, A6)

Mumbai's flashest cinema is set on the 2nd floor of the flashy CR-2 centre in Nariman Point. Five screens show a regularly-changing schedule of local blockbusters and imports, with buckets of popcorn available in the foyer. ☎ 56595959 ✉ 2nd flr, CR-2 Centre, Rajni Patel Marg, Nariman Point 💲 Rs 180-200 🚇 Churchgate

Regal Cinema (5, B1)

On SP Mukherji Chowk (Regal Circle), the Regal is one of Mumbai's classic Art Deco cinemas, and a charming place to catch a Bollywood *masala*

Deco classic: Regal Cinema

(song and dance spectacular) flick. It also screens the odd action film from Hollywood – usually with a much smaller audience. ☎ 22021017 ✉ SP Mukherji Chowk, Colaba 💲 Rs 40-150 🚇 Churchgate

Sterling Cinema (4, D2)

This smart air-conditioned cinema near Victoria Terminus (Chhatrapati Shivaji Terminus; CST) shows Indian blockbusters and pretty much anything with special effects from the USA. Hindi speakers can catch up with the latest from Bollywood in several theatres on the surrounding streets. ☎ 22075187 ✉ Marzaban Rd, Fort 💲 Rs 40-125 🚇 CST

PERFORMING ARTS

You can find listings of theatrical performances, concerts and dance in the free pamphlet *This Fortnight in Mumbai,* available from the India Tourism office (4, C3) near Churchgate station.

Bharatiya Vidya Bhavan (3, B3)

Established in 1938, this philanthropic organisation strives to preserve the knowledge of traditional Indian arts.

An interesting programme of lectures on Indian culture and philosophy takes place in the auditorium – call for details. ☎ 23631261 ✉ KM Munshi Marg, Chowpatty 🚇 Charni Road, Grant Road

Karnataka Sangh (1, A2)

Occasional free performances of Indian classical music and dance take place at this religious centre close to Matunga Road station. The schedule varies monthly – see *This Fortnight in Mumbai.* ☎ 24379645 ✉ M Vishweshwar Smarak Mandir, Kataria Rd, Mahim 🚇 Matunga Road

NCPA (3, C4)

A vast government-sponsored artistic complex on the waterfront at Nariman Point, the National Centre for the Performing Arts (NCPA) has a fast-changing schedule of theatre, music and traditional and contemporary performing arts. Look out for English-language plays, performances of Indian classical music and regional dance. ☎ 22833737 🖥 www.ncpa mumbai.com ✉ cnr Marine Dr & Shri V Saha Rd, Nariman Point 💲 tickets Rs 100-320 🕑 performances 6.30pm or 7pm 🚇 Churchgate

Nehru Centre Auditorium (3, B1)

The auditorium at the Nehru Centre shows occasional dance, theatre and music performances. Entry is free for most shows – call ahead or see *This Fortnight in Mumbai* for upcoming events. ☎ 24964680 ✉ Nehru Centre Auditorium,

Dr Annie Besant Rd, Worli
🚇 Mahalaxmi

Prithvi Theatre (2, A1)
This neighbourhood
theatre near Juhu Beach
is the leading performance
space for Hindi and Marathi
theatre in Mumbai. It also
puts on international and
local plays in English –
the website has the latest
schedule.
☎ 26149546 🖵 www
.prithvitheatre.org
✉ Janvi Kutir, Juhu Church
Rd, Juhu 💲 tickets Rs 50-
100, Sun Rs 150 🕑 shows
6pm & 9pm most evenings
🚇 Vile Parle

SPORT

As elsewhere on the sub-
continent, Mumbaikers are
cricket crazy. You can see in-
formal cricket matches any
day of the week on the Oval
and Azad Maidans in Fort.

**Mumbai Cricket
Association** (4, B3)
The Wankhede Stadium is
Mumbai's main venue for
cricket, and test and interstate matches attract huge
crowds. The main season is
September to April, but local
matches continue until July.
Contact the association in
advance to stand a chance of
obtaining test tickets.

Cricket crazy: practice at Brabourne Stadium

☎ 22819910 ✉ Wankhede
Stadium, D Rd, Churchgate
💲 local matches free,
interstate matches Rs
20, test matches Rs 50-
10,000 🕑 10am-5.30pm
🚇 Churchgate

**Royal Western India Turf
Club** (3, C1)
The Mahalaxmi Race Course
is regularly packed with
gamblers during the racing
season and the atmosphere
is frenzied and exhilarating. The racing season in
Mumbai runs from August
to April – at other times you
can bet on televised races
taking place elsewhere in
India. There's a requirement
that all mobile phones be
left with security to prevent
cheating.
☎ 23071401 🖵 www
.rwitc.com ✉ Mahalaxmi

Race Course, Keshavrao
Khadye Marg, Mahalaxmi
💲 admission Rs 20-150
🕑 2-5pm race days
🚇 Mahalaxmi

**Western India Football
Association** (5, A1)
Throughout Mumbai's
annual monsoon season
(June until October), both
amateur – and local – league
football matches are played
on the grass Cooperage
Football Ground, located in
northwestern Colaba. There
is no charge for entry to the
ground and you will find
watching other people
exert themselves is a very
pleasant way to while
away a few hours.
☎ 22024020 ✉ Cooperage
Football Ground, Maharshi
Karve Rd, Colaba 💲 free
🕑 4-6pm 🚇 Churchgate

KABADDI
One of the world's more unusual sports, kabaddi is played by two teams on a plain
dirt or grass court. In turn, a 'raider' from each team attempts to tag members of the
opposing team and return to their own side of the court, all the time chanting 'kabaddi,
kabaddi' on a single breath of air. Opponents try to catch the raider and hold them until
they take another breath. It's a popular diversion in Mumbai – the first ever Kabaddi
World Cup was held here in 2004. You can see matches on Sundays at **Shivaji Park**
(1, A2) on SV Savarkar Marg in Dadar.

SPECIAL EVENTS

January *Makar Sankranti* – Kite fights and festival food to celebrate the northern migration of the sun

Banganga Festival – Maharashtra Tourism Development Corporation–organised music festival at Banganga Tank (3, A3) on Malabar Hill

February–March *Holi (Rangapanchami)* – In this exuberant Hindu festival, locals throw around water and vast amounts of coloured powder to celebrate the end of winter – don't wear white!

Elephanta Festival – Classical music and dance performances on Elephanta Island (1, B3)

March–April *Muharram* – Model tombs are immersed in the sea at this Muslims commemoration of the martyrdom of Mohammed's grandson. Acts of ritual masochism are also performed

Gudi Padava – Maharashtran New Year, marked by the erection of *gudis* (poles decorated with colourful cloth and topped by an upturned pot)

June–August *Nag Panchami* – Snake charmers descend on Mumbai to honour Ananta, the serpent upon whose coils Vishnu rested

Nariyal Poornima – Koli communities offer coconuts and flowers to the sea god Varuna to calm the ocean at the end of the monsoon

Gokulashtami – Youths form human pyramids to reach pots filled with treats on tenement balconies in honour of Krishna's birthday

Pateti & Navroze – Mumbai's Zoroastrian community remember the flight from Persia by attending fire temples and feasting

August–September *Ganesh Chaturthi* – Mumbai's biggest festival sees thousands of clay images of Ganesh displayed in *pandals* (marquees) around town then ritually immersed in the sea at Chowpatty and other northern beaches; there's also music, dancing and water throwing

Bandra Fair – Feast day of the Virgin Mary, celebrated by all religions at the Basilica of Mount Mary (2, A3) in Bandra

September–October *Navratri (Dussehra)* – Celebration of Rama's victory over the demon king Ravanam, papier mâché demons are burned near Breach Candy's Mahalaxmi Mandir (3, B1)

Ramadan – Muslim month of daylight fasting, broken on the first sighting of the new moon at Id-ul-Fitr (moves back 11 days every year)

October–November *Diwali* – To celebrate Rama's return from exile, candles are lit in doorways and windows and children go on the offensive with firecrackers and fireworks

Kala Ghoda Fair – From November to February, K Dubash Marg goes arts, crafts and street-theatre crazy every Sunday

Jazz Yatra – Biennial jazz festival held in even-numbered years at various venues around the city

December *Christmas Day* – Christians in Colaba and Bandra decorate the streets with giant stars and attend midnight mass

New Year's Eve – Effigies of old men are paraded through the streets and set alight to mark the dying of the year

Sleeping

As a major shopping metropolis with a thriving tourist industry, Mumbai has plenty of accommodation. However, Mumbai's hotels charge some of the highest rates in India – and this doesn't always translate into good value for money. At the top end of the market you can find real luxury and Mumbai has no shortage of comfortable midrange accommodation, but the city is surprisingly bereft of cheap places to stay. If you're hoping to save money for shopping by staying in cheap hotels, think again.

Budget hotels in Mumbai are no worse than budget hotels elsewhere in India – most offer a bed in a small box-room with a ceiling fan and a choice of shared or private bathrooms – but few offer rooms for less than Rs 400 and many charge more than Rs 1000. Midrange hotels are usually a better bet and most offer spacious rooms with air-con, cable TV, phones, room service and attached bathrooms with hot showers. All hotels from midrange up accept major credit cards.

Moving upmarket, top-end hotels offer all the expected luxuries, including marble bathrooms, Internet connections, minibars and, of course,

> ## ROOM RATES
>
> Hotels are grouped according to the rates for a standard double room, but discounts of 20% to 30% are often available at top-end and deluxe hotels; ask when you book. Most top-end and deluxe hotels quote prices in US dollars.
>
> | | |
> |---|---|
> | deluxe | US$220 (Rs 9500) upwards |
> | top end | US$90 to US$220 (Rs 4000 to 9500) |
> | midrange | Rs 1500 to 4000 |
> | budget | Rs 250 to 1500 |

complimentary bathrobes and slippers. Top-end hotels invariably have attached restaurants, most serving top-class cuisine, and many also have pools, gyms and spas. If money is no object, Mumbai's deluxe hotels offer similar facilities with an extra touch of finesse.

The main tourist season runs from September to March, but most hotels charge the same rates year-round. Advance reservations are strongly recommended as hotels fill up fast. Budget hotels accept reservations without a deposit, but other hotels will ask for a credit-card advance, which you forfeit if you fail to turn up without cancelling the reservation. There's a useful hotel booking service at the **international airport** (☎ 56048772).

A doorman at the Taj Mahal Palace & Tower (p70)

DELUXE

Hilton Towers (3, C4)
Sharing a building with the Oberoi, the Hilton Towers lords over Nariman Point from its spot on Marine Dr (Netaji Subhashchandra Bose Marg). Facilities are glorious and the hotel boasts a massive arcade of swish boutiques and several of the city's finest restaurants. Expect water features, bowls of floating flowers and picture windows looking out over the ocean.
☎ 56324343 🖳 mumbai@trident-hilton.com ✉ Marine Dr, Nariman Point 🚇 Churchgate 🕭 excellent 🍴 India Jones (p59), Frangipani (p59) Opium Den (p62) 👶 babysitter available

JW Marriott (2, A1)
The palatial Marriott looks like an Arabian fortress dropped into the middle of Juhu Beach. The airy foyer is set around a lily pond and beachfront pool and the rooms contain everything the international executive might require, including a free teddy bear.
☎ 56933000 🖳 www .marriott.com/bomjw ✉ Juhu-Tara Rd, Juhu

🚇 Vile Parle 🕭 good 🍴 Lotus Café (p58), Mezzo Mezzo

Leela Kempinski (2, B1)
The Leela was always the grandest hotel in Mumbai, and the recent refurbishment has only lifted it higher. Traditional musicians play in a Mughal pavilion in the foyer and the rooms contain every imaginable luxury, including enormous plasma-screen TVs.
☎ 56911234 🖳 www .theleela.com ✉ Sahar Airport Rd, Sahar 🚇 Andheri or Vile Parle 🕭 good 🍴 Jamavar, Great Wall, Fiorella 👶 babysitter available

Orchid (2, B2)
Built according to strict ecological principles, the Orchid is surrounded by lush gardens, close to the domestic airport. Despite the location, it's a serene place, and everything is modern and understated. There's a rooftop pool and restaurant which will get you up above the city.
☎ 26164040 🖳 www .orchidhotel.com ✉ Nehru Rd, Domestic Airport, Vile Parle 🚇 Vile Parle 🕭 good 🍴 Mostly Grills, Vindhyas

Taj Mahal Palace & Tower (5, C2)
Mumbai's finest Raj hotel has been gracing the waterfront since 1903. The old building is a magnificent fantasy of arches, domes and towers, or you can stay high above the harbour in the modernist Taj Tower. Service runs to free afternoon cocktails and a complimentary bottle of wine in your room.
☎ 56653366 🖳 tmhresv .bom@tajhotels.com ✉ Apollo Bunder, Colaba 🚇 Churchgate 🕭 good 🍴 Golden Dragon (p50) 👶 babysitter available

TOP END

Ambassador (4, B4)
The glittering interior of the Ambassador could have been designed by an Indian Versace and the hotel is topped by Mumbai's only revolving restaurant. The glorious chintzy details extend into the rooms and you'll have the added satisfaction of staying in a Mumbai icon.
☎ 22041131 🖳 www.am bassadorindia.com ✉ Veer Nariman Rd, Churchgate 🚇 Churchgate 🕭 fair 🍴 Pearl of the Orient (p54), Society

Fariyas Hotel (5, A4)
An unexpected find in the residential area south of Arthur Bunder Rd, Fariyas Hotel is a smart modern tower hotel, with a small pool, a bar and restaurant and tastefully presented rooms with lush deep-pile carpets. Opt for an Executive Club room for the chance of a harbour view.

The glittering lobby of the Ambassador

THE HOTEL WITH THE MOSTEST

For the ultimate in luxury, head to the **ITC Grand Maratha Sheraton** (2, B1; ☎ 28303030; itcgrandmaratha.sales@welcomgroup.com; Sahar Airport Rd, Sahar; ☑ excellent) near the International Airport. The hotel boasts the best spa, the best restaurants and the best interior designer in Mumbai. Rooms feature wi-fi Internet, subtle lighting and sumptuous fabrics and you can titillate your taste buds at **Dakshin** (p59), **Pan-Asian** (p59) and **Peshawri** (p59), followed by a splash in the pool or a relaxing pummelling at the **Wellness Centre** (p47). Several rooms are specially designed for the disabled.

☎ 22042911 ☐ www
.fariyas.com ✉ D Vyas
Marg, Colaba ☒ Churchgate
☑ poor ✖ Abanara

☎ 22871122 ☐ www
.ghhotel.com ✉ 5 Battery
St, Colaba ☒ Churchgate
☑ poor ✖ All Stir Fry, Tides

Gordon House Hotel
(5, C1)
The most boutique of all Mumbai's boutique hotels, Gordon House offers three floors of stylish rooms with Scandinavian, Mediterranean and 'country cottage' themes. It's a little over the top, but the rooms are memorable and the facilities – including the popular Polly Esther's nightclub – are excellent.

Stylish Gordon House Hotel

Holiday Inn (2, A1)
The best of several hotels at the north end of Juhu Beach, the Holiday Inn is a classic 70s-style beach hotel with a beachside pool and a patio full of whispering palms. The building is slightly dated, but rooms have huge beds, sea views and wi-fi Internet access.
☎ 56934444 ☐ www
.holidayinnbombay.com
✉ Balraj Sahani Marg,
Juhu ☒ Vile Parle ☑ good
✖ Sampan, Bagicha

Hotel Marine Plaza
(4, A4)
More Miami than Mumbai, this glitzy hotel offers big hotel services on a boutique scale. Don't be put off by the clown prints in the lobby – there's an English-style pub, several restaurants, a fitness centre and a pool, and the rooms have soft carpets, bathtubs and fine sea views.
☎ 22851212 ☐ www
.sarovarparkplaza.com
✉ 29 Marine Dr, Church-

gate ☒ Churchgate ☑ fair
✖ Bayview, Oriental Blossom, Geoffrey's (p61)

Shalimar Hotel (3, B2)
Every inch the business hotel, the Shalimar is a short hop from Chowpatty Beach and Malabar Hill. You may find the bright-blue décor a bit much, but the air-conditioning is icy cold and the rooms provide a genuine haven from the busy streets outside.
☎ 56641000 ☐ www
.theshalimarhotel.com
✉ August Kranti Marg,
Breach Candy ☒ Grant Road
☑ poor ✖ Gulmurg

MIDRANGE

Ascot Hotel (5, A3)
Hidden behind a modest Art Deco façade, this stylish concept hotel is full of opaque glass, pale timber and cream-coloured marble. The futuristic rooms have every modern convenience and the bathrooms are gorgeous, with sunken bathtubs reached by marble steps.
☎ 5638 5566
☐ ascothotel@vsnl.com
✉ 38 Garden Rd, Colaba
☒ Churchgate ☑ fair

Hotel Bawa
International (2, B2)
The smartest midrange hotel at the domestic airport, Bawa International offers free airport transfers but it only takes five minutes to reach the check-in desks. You may need sunglasses for the brightly coloured rooms but facilities are excellent and the beds are piled with soft cushions.
☎ 26113636 ☐ www
.bawahotels.com ✉ Nehru

Rd, Domestic Airport, Vile Parle ⓡ Vile Parle, Andheri ♿ fair

Hotel Diplomat (5, B2)
Rooms at the Diplomat aren't quite as grand as you might expect, but this is still a good midrange choice. Spread over two buildings behind the Taj Mahal Palace & Tower, the rooms have fridges, TVs, tubs and comfy chairs, plus modest views over Colaba.
☎ 22021661 ⌨ www .hoteldiplomat-bombay.com ✉ 24/6 Mereweather Rd, Colaba ⓡ Churchgate ♿ none ✗ Indus (p62)

Hotel Sahar Garden (2, C1)
Close to the International Airport on MM Rd, this newly refurbished hotel offers free airport transfers and chintzy but cheerful rooms with air-con, TVs and black-marble bathtubs. Plane spotters should avail of the airport views from the upper rooms.
☎ 28500409
⌨ sahargarden@indiainfo .com ✉ MM Rd, Andheri ⓡ Vile Parle, Andheri ♿ none

Hotel Siddhartha (2, C3)
A recommended cheap choice for Bandra shoppers, Siddhartha offers friendly service and spacious rooms with unusual sofalike beds moulded into the walls. All rooms have TVs, phones, fridges and air-con and there's an on-site vegetarian restaurant.
☎ 26424326 ⌨ hotel -siddhartha@yahoo.com ✉ 368 SV Rd, Bandra ⓡ Bandra ♿ none ✗ Siddhartha Restaurant

Regent Hotel (5, B2)
The hotel of choice for visitors from the Persian Gulf, the Regent offers bright, colourful rooms in a handy location near Colaba Seafront. Rooms are full of Art Deco details and all have TVs, air-con, phones and fridges. Don't miss the free Arabian-style tea in the foyer.
☎ 22871853 ⌨ hotel regent@vsnl.com ✉ 8 Best Marg, Colaba ⓡ Churchgate ♿ none

Residency Hotel (4, D3)
Plenty of helpful staff lend a homely feel to this tidy business hotel in the middle of Fort. Rooms have TVs, phones, air-con, colourful curtains and floral prints on the walls, and there are several Parsi cafés nearby for a lunchtime dhansak (hot and sour curry with lentils).
☎ 56670555 ⌨ residency hotel@vsnl.com ✉ Rustom Sidhwa Marg, Fort ⓡ CST ♿ poor

Royal Inn (2, A2)
One of just a handful of hotels close to Linking Rd, Royal Inn is an excellent choice for well-heeled shopaholics. Rooms are compact but mirrors create the illusion of space and each has a TV, a minibar and a completely spotless marble bathroom.
☎ 26495151 ⌨ royal inn@vsnl.com ✉ cnr Khar Pali & Linking Rds, Bandra ⓡ Bandra ♿ none ✗ Sheetal Bukhara

Sea Green South Hotel (4, A4)
This unpretentious midrange place shares a building with the almost identical Sea Green Hotel on Marine Dr. The large tiled rooms have air-con, fridges and TVs and the sea views are the cheapest on the strip. If it's full, the rooms next door are just as good.
☎ 56336535 ⌨ www .seagreensouth.com ✉ 145A Marine Dr, Churchgate ⓡ Churchgate ♿ poor

Shelley's Hotel (5, B4)
Housed in an old 1930s apartment building on PJ Ramchandani Marg (Strand Rd), Shelley's is a charming leftover from the Raj. Rooms are unashamedly old fashioned, with tasteful hardwood furniture and miles of open floor space. For those in land-facing rooms, there are communal balconies with sea views on every floor.
☎ 22840229 ⌨ www .shelleyshotel.com ✉ 30 PJ Ramchandani Marg, Colaba ⓡ Churchgate ♿ fair ✗ Turquoise Restaurant

BUDGET

Bentley's Hotel (5, B3)
This friendly Parsi-run hotel is a Colaba institution and generations of travel writers have stayed here while writing Mumbai guides. Spread over several apartment buildings, the rooms are spick and span and all have TVs and optional air-con; it's all very white and calm and the staff is a genuinely friendly bunch.
☎ 22882890 ⌨ www .bentleyshotel.com ✉ 17 Oliver Rd, Colaba ⓡ Churchgate ♿ none

Bentley's Hotel (opposite): a calm, white haven

Gulf Hotel (5, B4)
One of several hotels targeting the Arabian tourism market, the Gulf is a palace of 1980s chintz. Still, the rooms are neat and uncomplicated and each floor has an air-conditioned lounge and a resident floor manager. Choose a deluxe room for a bathtub and fridge. ☎ 22856672 ⌨ info@gulf hotelmumbai.com ✉ Kamal Mansion, Arthur Bunder Rd, Colaba ⛆ Churchgate ♿ none

Hotel Lawrence (4, D5)
Hidden away in an anonymous office building on Sai Baba Marg (Rope Walk Lane) and reached by three cranky flights of stairs, Hotel Lawrence is simple, clean and cheap as chapatis. Bathrooms are shared but all rooms have fans and windows and the hotel is seconds from the eateries on K Dubash Marg (Rampart Row). ☎ 22843618 ✉ 33 Sai Baba Marg, Fort ⛆ Churchgate ♿ none

Hotel New Bengal (4, E1)
Probably the best bargain in Mumbai, this neat city hotel is Bengali owned and many guests are visiting traders from Kolkata. Appropriately, there's a Bengali restaurant on site and you can choose from clean box-rooms with shared bathroom or private

rooms with small en suites. ☎ 23401951 ⌨ www.bir yas.com ✉ Sitaram Bldg, Dr DN Rd, Fort ⛆ CST ♿ none ✗ Howrah (p53)

Iskcon Guest House (2, A1)
The mock-Mughal guest house at Juhu's Iskcon temple is completely over the top but rooms are decked out with Gujarati furniture and all have massive balconies. You don't need to be a Hare Krishna to stay here and there's a top-notch veg restaurant. ☎ 26206860 ⌨ guest .house.bombay@pamho.net ✉ Hare Krishna Land, Juhu Church Rd, Juhu ⛆ Vile Parle ♿ fair ✗ Govinda's (p58)

Sea Shore Hotel (5, B4)
The best of three cheap hotels in a single building near the waterfront, Sea Shore has good harbour views and rooms catch the

occasional sea breeze. Guests share three clean bathrooms and the hotel is staffed by an enthusiastic team of Game-boy players. Two rooms have air-con for an extra Rs 100. ☎ 22874237 ✉ Kamal Mansion, Arthur Bunder Rd, Colaba ⛆ Churchgate ♿ none

Welcome Hotel (4, F2)
Handy for Victoria Terminus (Chhatrapati Shivaji Terminus; CST) and the GPO, the Welcome is a pristine budget hotel, reached by marble steps. Rooms are impressively clean and rates include breakfast and snacks. Book ahead. ☎ 56314488 ⌨ welcome _hotel@vsnl.com ✉ 2nd flr, 257 Shahid Bhagat Singh Marg, Fort ⛆ CST ♿ none

YWCA (4, D6)
Perky staff, immaculate rooms and a free breakfast and newspaper in the morning make the YWCA one of the better choices in Fort. Men and women are welcome and guests have a choice of doubles or dorms. ☎ 22826814 ⌨ www .ywcaic.info ✉ 18 Madame Cama Rd, Fort ⛆ Churchgate ♿ none

QUICK ESCAPES
If you have an early flight or train out of Mumbai you may want to stay close to the station or airport. Here's a list of useful hotels for quick exits:

Welcome Hotel (right)	CST Train Station
Residency Hotel (opposite)	CST Train Station
Hotel Bawa International (p71)	Domestic Airport
Orchid (p70)	Domestic Airport
Hotel Sahar Garden (opposite)	International Airport
ITC Grand Maratha Sheraton (p71)	International Airport
Leela Kempinski (p70)	International Airport

About Mumbai

HISTORY
Sultans, the Portuguese & the British East India Company

The original inhabitants of the seven islands that make up Mumbai were Koli fishermen, but Hindu rulers swept down from the Deccan Plateau in around AD 500, establishing city states all along the Konkan Coast. By the 12th century a sizable Hindu dynasty was thriving on Mahim Island in north Mumbai.

From the beginning of the 14th century the islands fell under the influence of the Muslim Sultans of Gujarat and later the Portuguese, who established a base at Bassein in 1534. The islands passed to Britain in 1661 as part of the dowry of Catherine of Braganza, and were quickly sold to the British East India Company, which had been clamouring for a trading foothold on the Konkan Coast.

British Bombay

The undisputed father of British Bombay was Governor Gerald Aungier, who arrived here in 1672. Aungier established the judiciary, drained the malarial swamps, built the first docks and invited migrant workers from other parts of India to join the endeavour.

While all this was happening in Bombay, elsewhere on the coast Mughal sultanates were falling to the guerrilla army of Chhatrapati Shivaji Maharaj, founder of the Hindu Maratha kingdom. The governor of the British colony, Charles Boone, constructed Bombay Fort and merged the seven islands of Bombay into a single landmass.

In 1739 the Marathas drove the Portuguese from their base at Bassein and the British cleared the land in front of the fort as a defensive precaution, creating the Esplanade. Campaigns against the Portuguese and then the Marathas in 1817 finally brought most of western India under British control and the first railway in Asia was laid between Bombay and Thane in 1853.

Bombay's meteoric rise began in earnest in 1854, with the construction of the first cotton mills. Processing of Indian cotton shifted from Britain to Bombay and in 1857 Queen Victoria issued a declaration that Bombay was now a possession of the British Crown. Over the following decades, Jewish and Parsi entrepreneurs played a major role in establishing civic buildings and universities. In 1864 Governor Bartle Frere dismantled the Fort, creating the modern layout of Bombay.

As Bombay grew, it started to experience some of the big-city ills plaguing it today – overpopulation,

CHHATRAPATI SHIVAJI MAHARAJ

During the 1990s there were streets, museums, hospitals and airports all renamed in honour of Chhatrapati Shivaji Maharaj, the controversial hero of Mumbai's Maratha population. Born in 1627, Shivaji led a hugely successful campaign against the Mughal rulers of the Deccan, establishing a Hindu kingdom that lasted for 200 years. Unfortunately, naming things after Shivaji has a political dimension. Hindu nationalists see Shivaji as a freedom fighter while Muslims blame him for the demise of the Mughal empire.

poor sanitation and political unrest. Funded by the cotton mills, the Indian National Congress (later to become the Congress Party of India), held its first meeting in Bombay in 1885, sowing the seeds for Indian Independence.

Indian Rule

Despite economic advances like the creation of the Indian film industry in 1913, opposition to British rule grew steadily. Mahatma Gandhi took up residence on Laburnam Rd, launching his Quit India campaign in 1942. Bombay was barely touched by WWII, but by the time it was over it was apparent that the

Raj-era splendour at the Taj Mahal Palace & Tower (p70)

time had come for the British to leave. In 1947, they did.

After initial elation surrounding Independence, Bombay had to face up to some harsh realities. As capital of the state of Maharashtra, it ruled over two conflicting communities, the Gujarati speakers of the state's north and the Marathi speakers of the south. In 1960 the territory was divided into two separate states and divisions began to appear between the city's Hindu and Muslim populations.

Industrial disputes dominated the 1970s and 1980s. Many cotton mills closed, causing massive unemployment in working-class areas, and corruption permeated every aspect of political life. In 1985 control of the municipal council fell to the Hindu nationalist Shiv Sena party, which began actively stirring communal tensions.

Any pretence of communal harmony was blown apart in the violence that followed the destruction of the Ayodhya mosque (in Uttar Pradesh) in 1992. Hundreds of Hindus and Muslims died in intercommunal riots and bombings in Mumbai, blamed respectively on Shiv Sena agitators and Pakistan-backed militants.

A further wave of violence followed in 2003, when Islamic militants detonated car bombs at the Gateway of India and Zaveri Bazaar in Kalbadevi. There have been no major incidents since 2003 but community relations remain tense.

In June 2005 Maharashtra was devastated by flooding after the heaviest rains in Indian history. More than a thousand people died and 60,000 were left homeless, triggering fears of a new influx of refugees into Mumbai. The cost of the disaster has been estimated at US$1 billion, putting future plans for urban renewal in doubt.

ENVIRONMENT

Despite the urban sprawl, Mumbai is full of parks and pockets of wild forest. However, all are under threat from overpopulation and related pollution.

The waters around Mumbai are polluted with sewage from the slums and Mahim Creek is honking and black. Traffic pollution is another problem and urban development is threatening many remaining areas of wilderness.

Probably the most successful wild animal in Mumbai is the feral dog – the city has an estimated 40,000 of them. Populations of leopards in Sanjay Gandhi National Park (p35) were also on the increase until 2004, when 27 were caged following a spate of attacks. However, wild birds continue to flourish in the park.

Despite problems, there are some success stories. Polluting autorickshaws have been banned from the city centre and around a third of Mumbai's diesel taxis have been converted to Liquid Petroleum Gas (LPG).

GOVERNMENT & POLITICS

There are three tiers of government in Mumbai. The Brihanmumbai Municipal Council (BMC) handles city affairs, the Maharashtra Legislative Assembly and Council handles state affairs and six elected MPs represent Mumbai in Delhi.

Until recently Mumbai politics was dominated by the Shiv Sena, a Hindu nationalist party with links to intercommunal violence dating back to the 1960s. However, Congress regained control of the Legislative Assembly in the 2004 elections on a ticket of slum demolition and urban renewal.

The Shiv Sena continues to control the BMC and many Muslims still feel victimised by the organisation, which continues to exploit social and religious divisions. For its part, the Shiv Sena claims to be standing up for Hindus after centuries of Muslim oppression, which does little to help community relations.

HIGH-RISE LIVING

The skyline of Mumbai is dominated by tower blocks, but city planners now want to raise the city's profile even higher. With 60% of Mumbaikers living in slums due to Mumbai's extortionate real-estate prices, the Indian government has launched an ambitious plan to create a new city of Shanghai-style skyscrapers to halt the decay. However, urban renewal comes at a cost. To create space, the government has already cleared more than 90,000 shanties, leaving 300,000 people homeless.

ECONOMY

Mumbai was founded on the twin industries of shipping and cotton, but with the decline of the cotton mills, finance has become a major cash provider. The Bombay Stock Exchange and National Stock Exchange are both based here and call centres outsourced from Western nations are playing an increasingly important role in Mumbai's economy.

Mumbai Port is the busiest in India and the movie industry also brings in large amounts of revenue, though a staggering 80% of blockbusters fail

DID YOU KNOW?
- Mumbai's massive population of 16.4 million is less than 2% of India's total.
- The Bombay Stock Exchange is the oldest in India, established in 1875.
- There are 2145 suburban train services in Mumbai daily.
- More than 10% of India's mobile-phone users live in Mumbai.
- Sixty percent of Mumbai is built on reclaimed land.
- The average wage for unskilled workers in Mumbai is Rs 80 per day.
- Office space is more expensive in Mumbai than in downtown Manhattan.

to make a profit. However, unemployment currently stands at 600,000 people. Mumbai's economy is also held back by high office rents and low-level corruption, which keeps wealth predominantly in the hands of the Parsi and Gujarati communities.

The shop floor was traditionally dominated by Marathi speakers but many have shifted to white-collar work and moved out to the suburbs. Economic migrants from surrounding states continue to occupy the lowest positions.

SOCIETY & CULTURE

Mumbai has witnessed incredible changes over the last 50 years and there is a profound generational divide. Older Mumbaikers tend to be quietly traditional and slightly reserved, while younger Mumbaikers are cosmopolitan, forward thinking and inquisitive. Expect lots of questions about Western life from the young people you meet in cafés, bars and on public transport.

Although Mumbaikers are a progressive bunch, some things are still governed by tradition, particularly when it comes to relations between the sexes. Marriages are usually arranged by parents – albeit with increasing input from the bride and groom – and most people marry and socialise within their own caste or faith community. Mobile phones are currently causing a minor revolution in Indian dating, allowing youngsters to liberate their social lives from parental control.

Religion also plays an important role in the lives of Mumbaikers. Faith communities remain highly segregated and young people are easily roused by their religious leaders, as the riots and bombings of 1993 and 2003 demonstrated. Hindu nationalism is an ongoing issue for the Hindu community and some young Muslims are becoming radicalised by militant clerics.

Hinduism is followed by more than 75% of Mumbai's population, and most Hindus classify themselves as Shaivites (followers of Shiva) or Vaishnavites (followers of Vishnu). These loyalties dictate which temples and festivals are popular with different communities.

Muslims represent around 15% of the population and most are Sunnis, though Mumbai also has a small population of Bohra Shiites. Muslims remain one of the most disadvantaged communities in Mumbai, partly as a consequence of the biased social policies of the Hindu-dominated municipal council.

BAKSHEESH

Baksheesh used to mean a gratuity for services rendered, but these days it usually refers to alms for beggars and tips for unsolicited 'assistance'. Hangers-on are a problem in all tourist areas and if someone is getting on your nerves, you are quite entitled to tell them where to get off.

Begging is a harder situation to call. Some people give all the time. Some people never give on the basis that it creates dependency. If in doubt, a donation to a charity will probably help more than handing out cash in the street. Note that many beggars around Colaba are heroin addicts; hand-outs will do nothing to break the cycle of addiction.

Christians make up around 4% of the population and most are concentrated in former Koli areas such as south Colaba, Kotachiwadi and Bandra. Other important minorities include Sikhs, Buddhists, Jains and Parsis, who fled here in the 10th century to escape religious persecution in Iran. Mumbai also has a small community of around 3000 Bene and Sephardi Jews, originally from Judea and Syria. Jews and Parsis played a disproportionately large role for their numbers in the creation of modern Mumbai.

More recently, a new religion has emerged in Mumbai – shopping! The middle classes have gleefully embraced Western dress, Western liberal attitudes and the Western love of spending money. As a result, Mumbai is one of the best cities in India for shopping, socialising and nightlife. Predictably, the city is experiencing early symptoms of hyperconsumerism – novelty mobile-phone ring tones, obsession with brand-names and the like.

Etiquette

Despite its cosmopolitan outlook, Mumbai is still governed by strict social mores, most of them linked to religion. Immodest dress – ie anything that exposes the thighs or shoulders – meets with universal disapproval, though shorts and T-shirts are gaining popularity among the middle classes. Public displays of affection may also cause frowns.

Shaking hands – always with the right hand – is the standard greeting between men in Mumbai. Like most Asians, Mumbaikers prefer to avoid confrontation. Public arguments in particular are considered very bad form. If you take bargaining too seriously, everyone involved will lose face.

A few topics to avoid in conversation include Kashmir, the Babri Mosque and anything else that might inflame religious sentiments. Foreigners generally get a warm welcome in Muslim areas, but ask permission before entering mosques and remove your shoes before you enter.

When visiting Hindu temples and many churches, you should leave your shoes outside at the chappal (sandal) stand. Only a few Jain temples admit non-Jains and you must remove all leather items before you enter. Parsi *agiaries* (fire temples) and the Towers of Silence on Malabar Hill are off limits to non-Parsis.

Ask permission before taking photographs of local people – it's only polite and it can save you from awkward confrontations.

ARTS

Mumbai is rightly famous for its literature and cinema, but the city also has an impressive history of music, theatre, architecture and modern art. The JJ School of Art has produced some notable artists, including the painters SN Souza and SH Raza, who brought Indian art to a wider international audience. You can see top-quality modern art at many galleries in Mumbai (see p21).

Music in Mumbai means movie music, and the voices behind the songs in Bollywood blockbusters are celebrities in their own right. The most famous star of all is Lata Mangeshkar, the songbird behind an incredible 50,000 songs. Theatre is also growing in popularity – recently, attention has shifted from historical dramas to modern social commentary. See the Entertainment chapter for information on theatrical performances (p66).

Film

The film business in Mumbai began in 1913 with the production of the silent feature *Raja Harishchandra,* a historical epic with a cast of male actors in drag. Things took off quickly – by 1930 the Bombay film industry was producing more than 200 films per year. Talking pictures came to India the following year with the Imperial Film Company's *Alam Ara.* Within a year, films had been released in Bengali, Telugu and Tamil.

The public's appetite for movies was insatiable. Regional film industries sprung up across India, helped by the upsurge of interest in Indian culture after Independence. While Bengal became famous for art-house films, Bombay concentrated on popular entertainment. By the 1940s the *masala* formula had been created – risqué dance routines, rousing songs and epic locations, with a 'fighting injustice' or 'finding true love' plot fitted in somewhere between the big production numbers.

During the 1950s the studio system collapsed and independent producers moved in. By the 1970s the focus had shifted to ultraviolent

Presession buzz outside the Eros Cinema (p65)

action films, frequently starring Amitabh Bachchan. His 'one man against injustice' epic, *Sholay,* ran for an incredible six years at the Minerva Cinema on Grant Rd.

While the subjects for films have become more adventurous, the film industry remains highly censorious. The first screen kiss only sneaked onto the screen in 1978, and even today, love scenes rely mainly on clever camera angles and in- nuendo. That hasn't stopped a few controversial films slipping through – see the boxed text 'Dan- gerous Movies', above.

The term Bollywood was coined in the 1980s and the movie machine has been running on overdrive ever since, churning out nearly 100 films per month. See 'Bollywood or Bust' for more information (p20).

DANGEROUS MOVIES

Mumbaikers have been fascinated by the big screen ever since 1896, when the Lumiere Brothers' *Cinematographie* was shown at the Watson Hotel in Kala Ghoda. However, not all films have been quite so well received. Several movies have recently been pulled from cinemas after riots by outraged movie-goers, including the lesbian love story, *Girlfriend,* and the Sikh blockbuster, *Jo Bole So Nihaal,* which triggered a bombing campaign by Sikh hardliners. Another problem flick was Shyam Benegal's *Netaji Subhas Chandra Bose,* which outraged nationalists by suggesting that the Independence hero had secretly married a non-Indian.

Literature

Mumbai has always had a huge number of highly literate, highly educated citizens, so it should come as no surprise that the city is a hotbed of literary talent. In the early days the shining literary lights were British – Rudyard Kip- ling, of *Jungle Book* and *Just-So Stories* fame, was born here in 1865 – but attention later shifted to home-grown talents such as the Bene Jewish poet, Nissim Ezekiel. His *Collected Poems 1952-1988* remains some of the most evocative poetry ever written about the city.

Mumbai literature was launched onto the international scene by Salman Rushdie, regarded by many as India's finest writer. His novel *Midnight's Children,* an allegory for the experience of Indian Independence, won the Booker Prize in 1981. Mumbai features prominently in two later Rushdie novels, *The Moor's Last Sigh* and *The Ground Beneath Her Feet.*

Several authors have written movingly about the Parsi experience in Mumbai. Rohinton Mistry explored the complex relationships that form within a community inside a community in *Swimming Lessons & Other Stories from Firozsha Baag, Such a Long Journey* and *A Fine Bal- ance,* which is arguably the most biting book ever written about Indian politics.

Since the 1990s Mumbai itself has become the subject rather than simply the setting for books. Vikram Chandra presented his view of the city in five wry set pieces in *Love & Longing in Bombay.* More recently, Suketu Mehta penned the ultimate tribute to Mumbai in *Maximum City,* a work of love that explores the varied, frantic, sometimes brutal life of the city through the eyes of its inhabitants.

Directory

ARRIVAL & DEPARTURE

Mumbai is a major hub for domestic and international flights and plenty of cheap deals are available. Trains connect Mumbai to towns across India.

Air

Mumbai has two airports, the slightly dated **Chhatrapati Shivaji International Airport** (2, B2) and the newer **Santa Cruz Domestic Airport** (2, B2). Both airports have two terminals, one for Indian Airlines and Air India flights and one for all other airlines. Facilities at both airports include 24-hour left-luggage desks (p82), foreign exchange counters, ATMs, PCO/ISD phone booths, Internet cafés, shops and cafés.

INFORMATION

For information on either airport see the website www.bombayairport.com or call the following numbers.
International Inquiries (☎ 26829000)
Domestic Inquiries (☎ 26156600)
International Airport Hotel Booking Service (☎ 56048772)

AIRPORT ACCESS

A taxi is the easiest way to get to either airport – from central Mumbai, taxis charge a flat rate of Rs 350 for the one- to two-hour ride (see below for information on getting into town from the airport). If you have an early flight, ask your hotel to arrange a taxi for the morning. Alternatively, take the suburban train to Vile Parle and an auto-rickshaw from there (Rs 50). Free air shuttle buses link the international and domestic terminals.

International Airport

The prepaid taxi desk in the arrivals hall charges fixed rates – you'll pay Rs 110 to Juhu, Rs 200 to Bandra and Rs 325 to Colaba, plus Rs 10 per bag and Rs 5 service tax. You'll be given a receipt with a taxi number plate which you'll have to find in the car park. Air-con rates are 20% higher.

Domestic Airport

Taxis outside the domestic airport charge meter rates to the centre of town, plus Rs 10 per item of luggage. **Cool Cabs** (☎ 24905151) has air-con cabs to central Mumbai for around Rs 400.

Train

Central Railways (☎ 134) trains to the east and south (plus a few northern destinations) operate from **Victoria Terminus** (Chhatrapati Shivaji Terminus, CST; 3, E2) in Fort, while **Western Railways** (☎ 131) trains operate from **Mumbai Central Station** (3, C2) near Tardeo.

Trains out of Mumbai are often booked out days in advance, but a number of seats are set aside for tourists. To take advantage of the tourist quota, you should buy your tickets from the **Western Railways Reservations Office** (4, C3; ☎ 22635959; Maharshi Karve Rd, Churchgate) or the CST **Reservations Office** (☎ 22620079). Tickets can be purchased up to 60 days in advance and payment must be in US dollars, British pounds or Euros (cash or travellers cheques), or in rupees backed up by a foreign exchange receipt.

For non tourist-quota bookings, use the computerised reservation offices at the same locations. You can pay with Visa or MasterCard for a Rs 30 surcharge. All reservation counters are open 8am to 8pm Monday to Saturday and 8am to 2pm Sunday.

The following table shows rupee fares for journeys in two-tier and three-tier air-con carriages and fan-cooled sleeper carriages.

	Hours	2 tier	3 tier	Sleeper
Delhi	17-30	2210	1485	449
Chennai	26½	1673	1065	385
Goa (Panaji)	11	1242	796	293
Bangalore	24	1637	1043	381

Bus

Long-distance bus services depart from Mata Ramabai Ambedkar Marg (3, D3; behind Crawford Market) or Dr Anadrao Nair

Rd (3, D3; near CST). Private booths sell advance tickets to Goa, Bangalore, Hyderabad and other destinations in South India.

The following table shows rupee fares for normal and air-con bus journeys.

	Hours	Normal	Air-Con
Goa	16	350	550
Bangalore	24	500	1000
Hyderabad	16	350	700
Pune	4	150	200

Travel Documents
PASSPORT
Passports must be valid for at least six months at the time you apply for your visa.

VISA
Six-month multiple-entry tourist visas are issued to nationals of most countries. Fees vary with nationality; British citizens pay UK£30, American citizens pay US$30 and Australian citizens pay A$60. Note that Indian visas are valid from the date of issue, not the date of entry.

RETURN/ONWARD TICKET
Officials may ask to see a return or onward ticket when you apply for a visa.

Customs & Duty Free
Prohibited items include drugs (penalties are severe), plants and gold and silver bullion. Officially, Indian currency cannot be taken out of India, but this is rarely enforced. There are also restrictions on the export of some antiques, and items made from endangered animal species.

Visitors over 17 years can bring in the following items duty free: 200 cigarettes, 50 cigars or 250g of tobacco; 1L of alcohol and 250ml of perfume.

Left Luggage
Both airports have left-luggage offices in front of the terminals, open 24 hours. Rates are Rs 15 per item per day and bags must be locked. Photo ID is required to pick up your bags. Left-luggage offices at CST and Mumbai Central stations charge Rs 10 for the first 24 hours, Rs 12 for the next 24 hours and Rs 15 for each subsequent 24-hour period (train ticket required).

GETTING AROUND
To get from A to B with the minimum of fuss, flag down a cab. The only reason to use other forms of transport is a) for fun, and b) during morning and afternoon rush hour when the traffic is gridlocked.

In this book, the nearest train station is noted after the 🚇 in each listing. You may have to walk or take a taxi or autorickshaw to reach your destination.

Taxi
Based on a 1950s Fiat, Mumbai's black and yellow Premier taxis are by far the easiest way to get around. Drivers usually speak English and most are happy to use the meter. The fare is based on the meter reading and a complicated conversion chart, which all drivers carry. The minimum fare is Rs 13 for the first 1.6km and Rs 7 per kilometre thereafter. Rates go up by approximately 25% from midnight to 6am.

Note that taxis loitering outside tourist attractions and restaurants are usually looking for a long ride. Flag down a moving taxi for shorter journeys. See p81 for taxis to and from the domestic and international airports.

Train
Commuter trains to the suburbs leave from **CST** (Chhatrapati Shivaji Terminus/ Victoria Terminus; 4, E2; ☎ 22620746; Nagar Chowk, Fort) and **Churchgate** (4, B4; ☎ 22039840; Veer Nariman Rd, Churchgate). Passengers have a choice of padded seats in 1st class and bench seats in 2nd class. There are separate carriages for female travellers and the disabled. All classes are mobbed during the morning and evening rush hours, when passengers literally hang out of the doors.

COMPLICATED STREETS

Many streets in Mumbai have two names, an older, British colonial name and a post-Independence Indian name (see the table below). Some of the 'new' official names are used widely, others are ignored by everyone except municipal cartographers, and some are used interchangeably, including on street signs and business cards. To make things more complicated, street names are often abbreviated – for example, Mahatma Gandhi Rd is usually known as MG Rd and Dr Dadabhai Nawrojee Rd is almost always known as Dr DN Rd. In this book, we have followed the most commonly used name in the text, but the more frequently used alternative names are listed in brackets on the maps and at the first mention in each chapter.

New Name	Old Name
Chhatrapati Shivaji Marg	Apollo Bunder Rd
August Kranti Marg	Gowalia Tank Rd
Best Marg	Ormiston Rd
Bhulabhai Desai Rd	Warden Rd
Dr Dadabhai Nawrojee (DN) Rd	Hornby Rd
Dr Gopalrao Deshmukh Marg	Peddar Rd
Guru Nanak Rd	Turner Rd
Hutatma Chowk	Flora Fountain
K Dubash Marg	Rampart Row
L Jagmohandas Marg	Nepean Sea Rd
Lokmanya Tilak Marg	Carnac Rd
Mahakavi Bhushan Marg	Lansdowne Rd
Maharshi Karve Rd	Queen's Rd
Maulana Shaukatali Rd	Grant Rd
Mata Ramabai Ambedkar (MRA) Marg	Paltan Rd
Mumbai Samachar Marg	Apollo St
Nathalal Parekh Marg	Wodehouse Rd
Netaji Subhashchandra Bose Marg	Marine Dr
Nyayamurti Sitaram Patkan Marg	Hughes Rd
Pathe Bapurao Marg	Falkland Rd
PJ Ramchandani Marg	Strand Rd
Prakash Pethe Marg	Cuffe Pde
Rammohan Roy Marg	Charni Rd
RK Patkar Marg	Waterfield Rd
Rustom Sidhwa Marg	Gunbow St
Sai Baba Marg	Rope Walk Lane
Salebhai Karimji Badodawala Marg	Altamount Rd
Shahid Bhagat Singh Marg	Colaba Causeway
Sir V Thackersay Marg	New Marine Lines
SK Chandra Rd	Hill Rd
SP Mukherji Chowk	Regal Circle
S Vivekanand Marg	Ghodbunder Rd
SV Patel Marg	Sandhurst Rd

Start at Churchgate for Charni Road (Chowpatty), Mumbai Central (for long-distance buses and trains), Mahalaxmi (dhobi ghats and Haji Ali), Lower Parel (Phoenix Mills Shopping Centre), Bandra, Vile Parle (Juhu and airports) and Borivali (Sanjay Gandhi National Park). Take the 'slow train' for stations before Bandra. Fares range from Rs 41 to 180 in 1st class and Rs 5 to 24 in 2nd class.

Bus

Single- and double-decker buses run all over the city, but routes are confusing and there's a mad rush to get off at every stop. For more information, contact **BEST Undertaking** (5, A2; ☎ 22185541; www.bestundertaking.com; Colaba Bus Depot, Colaba Causeway, Colaba).

Autorickshaw

North of Mahim Creek, autorickshaws do the job of taxis. Rates are similar to taxis but you may have to bargain as drivers are less inclined to use the meter.

Car & Motorcycle

The best option for long-distance travel is to hire a taxi with a driver – contact India Tourism (p89) for more information. If you prefer to drive yourself, try **Avis** (3, C4; ☎ 22857518; Oberoi Hotel, Nariman Point).

PRACTICALITIES
Business Hours

Offices 9.30am-5.30pm Mon-Fri
Shops 10am-7pm Mon-Sat
Banks 10.30am-4.30pm Mon-Fri, 10.30am-1.30pm Sat
Foreign Exchange Centres 9.30am-6.30pm Mon-Sat

Climate & When to Go

Mumbai is warm and humid year-round, but there are three distinct seasons: winter (October to February) summer (March to June) and the monsoon (June to October).

By far the most pleasant time to visit is in winter, when temperatures are moderate and the skies are clear. From March, temperatures start to soar and the humidity can become unbearable.

The monsoon sees incredible amounts of rain bucket down on Mumbai and flooding is common. Some attractions and tours stop running but there are some fascinating festivals during this time, including Ganesh Chaturthi – see the Special Events box (p68).

Disabled Travellers

Mumbai is not well set up for disabled travellers. Most hotels, restaurants and attractions have steps, lifts stop between floors, pavements are uneven, disabled ramps are nonexistent and taxis have little space for wheelchairs. Wheelchair users in Mumbai will benefit from a strong, able-bodied companion to help with boarding taxis, buses and trains, which have a small disabled carriage.

Discounts

Children – generally defined as under 12 years of age – get discounts on public transport and on entry to most tourist attractions. Under fives are usually free. Concessions are provided for the elderly at a handful of attractions.

Electricity

Electricity supplies are generally reliable, but power cuts are not uncommon during the monsoon.
Voltage 230-240V
Frequency 50 cycles
Plugs 2 or 3 round pins

Consulates & High Commissions

Foreign consulates and high commissions in Mumbai:

Australian Consulate (4, A6; ☎ 56692000; 3rd fl, Makar VI Bldg, Jamnalal Bajaj Marg, Nariman Point)

British Consulate (4, A6; ☎ 56502222; 2nd fl, Maker IV Bldg, Jamnalal Bajaj Marg, Nariman Point)

Canadian Consulate (4, A6; ☎ 22876027; 4th fl, Makar VI Bldg, Jamnalal Bajaj Marg, Nariman Point)

French Consulate (4, A6; ☎ 56314000; 7th fl, Hoescht House, Vinayak K Shah Rd, Nariman Point)

German Consulate (4, A6; ☎ 22832422; 10th fl, Hoescht House, Vinayak K Shah Rd, Nariman Point)

Italian Consulate (3, B2; ☎ 23804071; 72 Peddar Rd, Breach Candy)

Spanish Consulate (4, D5; ☎ 22871089; Ador House, 3rd fl, 6 K Dubash Marg, Fort)

US Consulate (3, B2; ☎ 23633611; 78 Bhulabhai Desai Marg, Breach Candy)

Emergencies

Crime is not a major problem for visitors to Mumbai, though petty theft and scams are reasonably common. Pickpockets can be a problem on public transport and at crowded tourist attractions – keep an eye on your valuables! As in any big city, women should avoid walking around alone late at night. Intercommunal violence is a problem in Mumbai – avoid demonstrations and other potential flashpoints.

Ambulance ☎ 102
Fire ☎ 101
Police ☎ 100

Fitness
GOLF

There is only one choice for golfers in Mumbai, the exclusive **Bombay Presidency Golf Club** (1, B2; ☎ 25505874; Dr C Gidwani Rd, Chembur). The 18-hole course is open Tuesday to Sunday and green fees are Rs 1000 on weekdays and Rs 1200 at weekends.

GYMS

Unless your hotel has a gym, you'll have to join a private gym for a month-long membership fee of around Rs 3500. The following gyms are well equipped:

Inch by Inch (4, A1; ☎ 22828884; 95 Parijat Bldg, Marine Dr, Churchgate; ⊙ 6am-10pm Mon-Fri, 8am-4pm Sat & Sun)

Talwalkars (3, B2; ☎ 23636406; Khatau Mansion, 95 Bhulabhai Desai Marg, Breach Candy; ⊙ 10am-8pm)

SWIMMING

Swimmers in Mumbai have the choice of hotel pools, the sea or several water-based theme parks in the suburbs – see Sights & Activities chapter for details (p31). A few hotel pools accept nonguests for a fee of around Rs 500.

Fariyas Hotel (5, A4; ☎ 22042911; D Vyas Marg, Colaba)

Orchid (2, B2; ☎ 26164040; Nehru Rd, Domestic Airport, Andheri)

Ramada Plaza Palm Grove (2, A1; ☎ 26112323; Juhu-Tara Rd, Juhu)

YOGA

Most yoga centres prefer long-term students. **Kaivalyadhama** (3, C3; ☎ 22818417; www.kdham.com; 43 Marine Dr, Chowpatty) may accept experienced practitioners at some of its weekly classes – call for details.

Gay & Lesbian Travellers

Homosexual sex between men is illegal in India under Section 377 of the national legislature but that doesn't stop Mumbai having a small, extremely low-profile gay scene. Lesbianism is not illegal, but there is no formal scene.

Because of the legal and social implications of homosexuality in India, gay life generally takes place behind closed doors. There is just one gay night in town:

Saturday night at the **Voodoo Pub** (p64) in Colaba.

The organisation **Gay Bombay** (www .gaybombay.com) organises occasional gay events at venues around the city – the website has listings and other gay resources. Another useful organisation is the **Humsafar Trust** (☎ 26187476; www.humsafar .org; 2nd fl, Vakola Muncipal Bldg, Nehru Rd, Santa Cruz), which runs a helpline and drop-in centre in Santa Cruz.

Despite Mumbai's progressive attitudes, public affection is frowned on for both straight and gay couples. Straight Indian men often hold hands as a sign of friendship, but foreign men holding hands may well attract attention.

Health
IMMUNISATIONS
No immunisations are currently required for Mumbai and malaria is not regarded as a serious risk. If you are visiting from an affected area in Africa or South America, you may need a yellow fever vaccination.

PRECAUTIONS
Avoid drinking or brushing your teeth with tap water, peel or wash fruit, clean your hands regularly and only eat street food that you see prepared freshly in front of you. Fruit juices prepared with water or ice are particularly risky, as are salads, though the *bhelpuri* (Mumbai-style salad) served at Chowpatty Beach is usually safe. Bottled purified water is available everywhere – dispose of plastic water bottles responsibly. Be alert to dehydration, sunstroke, heat exhaustion and prickly heat.

MEDICAL SERVICES
For minor health problems, visit a pharmacist or contact India Tourism (p89) for a list of doctors. Foreigners normally pay Rs 100 to 200 for a consultation.

For anything serious, the following hospitals have 24-hour accident and emergency services.

Bombay Hospital (4, C1; ☎ 22067676; New Marine Lines, Churchgate)
Saifee Hospital (3, C3; ☎ 23861418; Charni Rd, Girgaum)
St George's Hospital (4, F1; ☎ 22620344; P D'Mello Rd, Fort)

PHARMACIES
There are pharmacies all over Mumbai where you can buy common medicines without a prescription.
Bombay Hospital Pharmacy (4, B1; ☎ 22067676; Bombay Hospital, New Marine Lines, Churchgate; ☷ 24 hr)
Colaba Chemist (5, A4; ☎ 22834301; cnr Arthur Bunder Rd & Colaba Causeway, Colaba; ☷ 8am-11pm)

DENTAL SERVICES & OPTICIANS
For emergency dental treatment, try the **Government Dental College & Hospital** (4, F1; ☎ 22620668; St George's Hospital Compound, P D'Mello Rd, Fort; ☷ 8.30am-4pm Mon-Fri, 2nd & 4th Sat).

For replacement glasses and contact lenses, try **Lawrence & Mayo** (4, D3; ☎ 22076049; 274 Dr DN Rd, Fort; ☷ 10am-7.30pm Mon-Sat).

Holidays
As well as the following secular public holidays, many offices and shops close for important religious festivals (see p68).
New Year's Day 1 January
Republic Day 26 January
Good Friday March/April
Dr Ambedkar's Birthday 14 April
Maharashtra Day 1 May
Independence Day 15 August
Mahatma Gandhi's Birthday 2 October

Internet
Internet access is widely available in Mumbai, though locals use the web mainly for chat. Deluxe and top-end hotels offer in-room Internet access – often wi-fi – and there are net cafés at the domestic and international airports.

INTERNET SERVICE PROVIDERS

AOL (www.aol.com) is one of the few international service providers with a local dial-up node (☎ 56490296, 56419700). Local Internet service providers include **MTNL** (www.mtnl.net.in), **Satyam Infoway** (www.sify.com) and **VSNL** (www.vsnl.com).

INTERNET CAFÉS

Net cafés in Mumbai charge Rs 20 to 35 per hour. The following are reliable options:

Waghela Communications Centre (5, B2; ☎ 22048718; 23B Narowji F Rd, Colaba; ☼ 8.30am-midnight)

Portasia (4, D3; ☎ 22037292; 192 Dr DN Rd, Fort; ☼ 9am-9pm)

Surf Dragonz (2, C2; ☎ 56939385; 246 Waterfield Rd, Bandra; ☼ 10am-midnight)

USEFUL SITES

The Lonely Planet website (www.lonelyplanet.com) offers a speedy link to many of Mumbai's websites. Other useful sites:

Mumbai on the Net (www.mumbainet.com)

Mumbai Hub (www.mumbaihub.com)

Mumbai Central (www.mumbai-central.com)

Mumbai Airport (www.mumbaiairport.com)

Metric System

India adopted the metric system in 1956 so fruit is sold in kilograms and distances are measured in kilometres. Premetric measurements still in use include crore (10 million) and lakh (100,000).

Money

See also Tipping & Bargaining (p89).

ATMS

Most banks have ATMs that accept Visa, MasterCard and other major international credit cards – bank head offices are on Dr DN Rd in Fort. In Colaba, there are ATMs at Citibank on SP Mukherji Chowk (Regal Circle) and at the State Bank on Mandlik Rd.

CHANGING MONEY

Banks and foreign exchange offices offer similar rates and commissions – typically 1% on each transaction. The **State Bank of India** (4, E4; ☎ 22661765; Bank St, Fort; ☼ 10.30am-4.30pm Mon-Fri, 10.30am-1.30pm Sat) changes cash and travellers cheques (Amex, Thomas Cook, Visa and Citibank) in most major currencies.

The following are reliable foreign exchange offices:

American Express (5, C1; ☎ 56385404; Regal Cinema Bldg, Chhatrapati Shivaji Marg, Colaba; ☼ 9.30am-6.30pm Mon-Fri, 9.30am-2.30pm Sat)

LKP (5, A4; ☎ 22882517; 22B Cusrow Baug, Colaba Causeway, Colaba; ☼ 9.30am-6.30pm Mon-Sat) Has a branch on Sitaram Patkar Marg, Chowpatty (3, B3).

Thomas Cook (4, D3; ☎ 22048556; Dr DN Rd, Fort; ☼ 9.30am-6.30am Mon-Sat)

CREDIT CARDS

Visa, MasterCard/Maestro and American Express (Amex) cards are accepted by tourist shops, upmarket restaurants and most midrange, top-end and deluxe hotels. For 24-hour card cancellations or assistance:

Visa (☎ 0001178666700955)

MasterCard/Maestro (☎ 0016367227111)

American Express (☎ 1600331245)

CURRENCY

The unit of currency is the Indian rupee, made up of 100 paise. There are coins of one, two and five rupees and notes of one, two, five, 10, 20, 50, 100, 500 and 1000 rupees. If you have a damaged note, take it to the State Bank of India (above).

TRAVELLERS CHEQUES

Travellers cheques are a useful backup – rates are similar for cash and cheques and major brands of travellers cheque are accepted at banks and moneychangers.

Newspapers & Magazines

Mumbai has lively and opinionated daily press, exemplified by the broadsheet *Times of India* and the tabloid *Mid-Day*. For information on entertainment and dining, pick up the Mumbai edition of *Time Out*. The Bollywood scene is explored with zeal in *Stardust, Filmfare* and *Cineblitz*. International newspapers and magazines are available from larger bookshops – see Shopping (p44).

Photography & Video

Print and slide film, PAL-format video cassettes and cards for digital cameras are widely available in Mumbai. Several shops opposite Victoria Terminus sell photographic supplies and offer printing and processing – try **Standard Supply Co** (4, E2; ☎ 22612468; 123 Walchand Hirachand Marg, Fort; ☺ 10am-7pm Mon-Sat).

Post

For stamps and postal services, head to the **General Post Office** (GPO; 3, F2; Walchand Hirachand Marg, Fort; 10am-8pm Mon-Sat). Parcels are handled by the **parcel office** (4, F2) on the 3rd floor of the annexe behind the GPO. For couriers:
Blue Dart (4, E2; ☎ 22695964; 28/32 Mint Rd, Fort; ☺ 8am-9pm Mon-Sat)
DHL (4, A4; ☎ 30300345; Sea Green Hotel, 145A Marine Dr, Churchgate; ☺ 8am-10pm Mon-Sat, 8am-2pm Sun)

POSTAL RATES

Postcards cost Rs 4 within South Asia and Rs 6 to 7 to the rest of the world. Letters cost from Rs 7 in India or Rs 9 to 11 worldwide. International airmail parcels (up to 20kg) cost Rs 375 to 485 for the first 250g and Rs 45 to 90 for each additional 250g.

Radio

Most radio stations broadcast in multiple languages. Stations with English-language content include **Go 92.5FM** (92.5FM), **Radio Mirchi** (98.3FM), **All India Radio** (1044AM) and the **BBC World Service** (15310/17790 Shortwave).

Telephone

Mumbai has hundreds of tiny PCO/ISD/STD centres where you can make local and international calls at a digitally metered rate. Avoid making calls from your hotel room – you'll pay four or five times the going rate.

For after-hours calls, head to the **Central Telegraph Office** (4, C4; Veer Nariman Rd, Fort; ☺ 24hr) near Flora Fountain.

MOBILE PHONES

Mobile phone numbers in Mumbai are normally prefixed ☎ 98. People with GSM phones with 'global roaming' can connect to the Orange Mumbai and BPL Mobile networks. Both companies offer prepaid SIM-card packages for Rs 500. Talk-time cards are sold at phone offices and Internet cafés.

COUNTRY & CITY CODES

The country code for India is ☎ 91 and the city code is ☎ 022 (drop the zero if calling from abroad).

USEFUL PHONE NUMBERS

Local Directory Inquiries (☎ 197)
International Direct Dial Code (☎ 00)
International Directory Inquiries (☎ 187)
International Operator (☎ 186)
Time (☎ 174)

Television

Any hotel rooms with TVs will show cable or satellite channels, usually from the Star or Zee networks, which both have English-language movie channels and BBC or CNN international news.

Time

Like the rest of India, Mumbai is 5½ hours ahead of GMT/UTC, 4½ hours behind Australian Eastern Standard Time and 10½ hours ahead of American Eastern Standard Time. Daylight saving time is not used.

Tipping & Bargaining

Tipping is not required in cheaper restaurants or in taxi cabs. Posher restaurants and upmarket hotels generally add a service charge of 10% to the bill. It is usual to tip hotel staff and porters for carrying bags.

Bargaining is usually only necessary at street stalls and in tourist shops; other shops generally have fixed prices. If you do intend to bargain, start by offering 50% of the asking price and move up in small increments until you and the seller reach a satisfactory price.

Toilets

Indian-style squat toilets are a simple hole in the ground and wiping – or rather washing – is done with a jug of water and the left hand. Most hotels and restaurants in Mumbai have Western-style 'sit-down' toilets and toilet tissue. Public toilets in Mumbai are a fright; if you get caught short, duck into a restaurant or coffee shop.

Tourist Information

India Tourism (4, C3; ☎ 22074333; www .india-tourism.com; 2nd fl, Western Railway Reservations Office, Maharshi Karve Rd, Churchgate; ☽ 8.30am-6pm Mon-Fri, 8.30am-2pm Sat) is knowledgeable about the whole of India and staff have stacks of information about Mumbai.

The **MTDC** (Maharashtra Tourism Development Corporation; 3, A5; ☎ 22024482; ☽ 9.45am-5.30pm Mon-Sat) basically exists to promote tours to other parts of Maharashtra but it can provide limited local advice.

Women Travellers

Mumbai is one of the most emancipated cities in India and women are appearing in more and more positions of power. Nevertheless, solo female travellers may still face unsolicited attention. A polite but firm rebuttal is usually enough, but avoiding 'immodest' dress – anything that exposes the thighs, stomach or shoulders – will help. Tampons are available from Western-style chemists but contraceptive pills should be brought from home.

LANGUAGE

Mumbai has two official languages – English and Marathi. Most Mumbaikers speak Hindi, and Gujarati is quite common among the Muslim community. Most people will understand if you talk slowly and clearly in English. For an English-speaking guide, contact India Tourism (p37).

Index

See also separate indexes for Eating (p93), Entertainment (p94), Shopping (p94), Sleeping (p94) and Sights with map references (p94).

FEATURES
Apoorva .... *Eating*
Sterling Cinema .... *Entertainment*
Toto's Garage .... *Drinking*
Insomnia .... *Café*
Mani Bhavan .... *Highlights*
Fab India .... *Shopping*
Museum Art Gallery ...... *Sights/Activities*
Hotel Lawrence .... *Sleeping*

AREAS
.... Beach, Desert
.... Building
.... Land
.... Mall
.... Other Area
.... Park/Cemetery
.... Rocks
.... Sports

HYDROGRAPHY
.... River, Creek
.... Intermittent River
.... Mudflats
.... Swamp
.... Water

ROUTES
.... Tollway
.... Freeway
.... Primary Road
.... Secondary Road
.... Tertiary Road
.... Lane
.... Under Construction
.... One-Way Street
.... Mall/Steps
.... Tunnel
.... Walking Path
.... Walking Trail/Track
.... Pedestrian Overpass
.... Walking Tour

TRANSPORT
.... Airport, Airfield
.... Bus Route
.... Ferry
.... Rail

BOUNDARIES
.... State, Provincial

SYMBOLS
.... Beach
.... Buddhist
.... Castle, Fortress
.... Bank, ATM
.... Christian
.... Diving, Snorkelling
.... Embassy, Consulate
.... Hospital, Clinic
.... Hindu
.... Jain
.... Information
.... Internet Access
.... Islamic
.... Monument
.... Point of Interest
.... Police Station
.... Post Office
.... Ruin
.... Shinto
.... Sikh
.... Swimming Pool
.... Trail Head
.... Wheelchair Access

24/7 travel advice
www.lonelyplanet.com